SEASONAL STORYTELLING

A CALENDAR OF STORY, DRAMA, DANCE AND SONG

ILLUSTRATIONS BY KRISTY BARLOW

TANYA BATT

All songs/stories/chants/foot stories are authored by Tanya Batt unless otherwise stated.
Throughout this book the symbol (♪) indicates that there is a recording available of the indicated
song or story. Please scan this QR to access these recordings.

Tipi Press,
an imprint of Lasavia Publishing Ltd.
Auckland, New Zealand

www.lasaviapublishing.com

ISBN: 978-1-991083-19-7

For the ancestors of the lands we live on
and the lands we came from,
and the future generations
who will plant the seeds.

CONTENTS

INTRODUCTION

SUMMER – RAUMATI

AUTUMN – NGAHURU

WINTER – HŌTOKE

SPRING – KŌANGA

APPENDIX

ACKNOWLEDGEMENTS

Ngā mihi nui to Kristy Barlow for her beautiful illustrations that breathe colour into this resource and to Vibeke Brethouwer for suggesting I pull the material together into a book. I'm grateful for the support from my wider community, family and friends that allowed me to take up a writer's residency in 'The Church' in Rawene to work on the manuscript, and the many kindnesses shown to me by my partner Peter Forster. Thanks to Linda Blincko and Lynn Lawton whose dreams have afforded the residency opportunity to artists. Ngā mihi to Debbie Upham, Fiona Collins, Heather Knewstubb and Moira Wairama for taking the time to read the manuscript and give feedback. Ngā mihi nui to Maikara Ropata whose kind and knowledgeable eyes checked my reo, to Puti Pere, my first kaiako of te reo and tikanga (Auckland Teacher College 1991 – 1993) and for the ongoing support and learning opportunities I receive through my studies with Te Wananga O Aotearoa. Thank you to Juliet Batten, whose long-standing work in this field has been a source of confirmation and inspiration. And finally thanks to Lasavia Publishing for taking on this project – Rowan Johnson and Daniela Gast – for their skills in editing and designing the book that you're now able to enjoy.

INTRODUCTION

Mā te whakarongo, ka mōhio,

mā te mōhio, ka mārama,

mā te mārama, ka mātau,

mā te mātau, ka ora.

Through paying attention, comes knowledge,

through knowledge, comes understanding,

through understanding, comes wisdom,

through wisdom, comes wellbeing.

– Pā Henare Tate

LIVE EACH SEASON AS IT PASSES;
BREATHE THE AIR, DRINK THE DRINK, TASTE THE FRUIT, AND
RESIGN YOURSELF.

– HENRY DAVID THOREAU

There is some irony in writing a book encouraging seasonal celebrations at a time when our seasons are becoming increasingly unpredictable with the effects of climate change. Perhaps climate change could be embraced as a planetary call to pay more attention to our surroundings. If so, this resource echoes that call in encouraging people to embrace the changes in our environments, as a teacher.

My whakapapa is largely northern and like the many people from the northern hemisphere who came to call the Antipodes home, my ancestors brought their values, beliefs and northern calendar with them. I write this resource from this perspective. I was born in Aotearoa New Zealand and grew up in Australia, celebrating spring festivals in autumn and eating shared midwinter feasts during the height of summer. The 'we' I will often speak of, are those who share a similar story.

As someone who has always loved stories, I have also always loved celebrations. Our cultural celebrations are the embodiment of our stories. In its simplest form, culture is created by a group of people believing/participating in shared stories.

One of my objectives as a storyteller is to reawaken an awareness of the lost stories that inform many celebrations. When we lose knowledge of our stories that in turn give meaning to our celebrations, a vacuum is created and celebrations become superficial. They become focused on what we can buy and how things look and reverence is often diminished or lost.

Storytelling has long been instrumental in developing a sense of connection amongst people and to place. As a gardener who lives by the changing seasons, I quickly became aware that even when an awareness of the origins of stories is reseeded, many of these stories are anchored to other lands.

For all immigrants there is a fine line between the importance of preserving traditions, knowledge and connections to our ancestral homes and that of colonising a landscape with preconceived ideas. These often fail to acknowledge and respect indigenous people and their knowledge, and erode an appreciation of the environment that we are now part of. It is not unusual to try and recreate what is familiar, but it can result in failure to see and value the uniqueness of the new environment.

This collection of stories, songs, dances and activities was created with the intention of consciously realigning northern celebrations and stories with the seasons of the southern hemisphere, acknowledging mātauranga Māori and reconnecting with the whenua, the land that we are fortunate to have come to know as home. I want to create a fusion between tradition reimagined, the reality of what is actually happening in our immediate environment, and recognition and respect for wisdom that comes from being part of a place for the longest time.

The concept of the four seasons, spring, summer, autumn and winter is not a universal framework. All cultures have their own way of marking time that is very specific to their observed/experienced environment. Some people have several seasons; some calendars are celestially guided; some pay equal attention to the solar and lunar cycles. The great gift of diversity is the realisation that there is not just one way to understand the world.

The English word, 'calendar' takes its origins from the Latin word, 'calare' which means to 'solemnly call out'. Time was not calculated or predetermined, but observed by priests of old Rome, who then 'called out' those observations to the wider community. While the word calendar now often refers to dates printed in a diary and celestial configurations, it's in fact what is 'calling out' to you from outside your door, in your garden and the places you call home.

This wisdom is inherent in the maramataka of te ao Māori. Guided by the cycles of the moon,

and other celestial movements, there is no singular all-encompassing calendar – every region has its own calendar, relevant to the immediate ecology and the local tohu/signs. One of the tohu/signs of spring for me at Awaawaroa on Waiheke Island is the Bell frogs, 'calling out' from the garden pond. This usually begins towards the end of August, rarely on exactly the same date, each year.

I will be using the four seasons to structure this resource, as it is a concept many people are familiar with. Many of my references relate specifically to Aotearoa/New Zealand and the mātauranga/knowledge of the first nations people of this land, tangata Māori. I do not whakapapa Māori and so what I refer to in this resource is what I've been fortunate enough to learn from tangata Māori who are friends or colleagues, through courses of study I have taken (and continue to do so) in tikanga and te reo Māori and what is shared in the public domain (books, on the internet, in public spaces). I share this mātauranga in acknowledgement of tangata Māori as the first humans to live and die on this land and to know deeply her moods and seasons in a way that can only be forged by time.

I encourage anyone reading this to take direction from your immediate environment and those who have been connected to the land you work/live on for the longest time. Enquire gently for directions amongst the families of the children you work with and your wider community and be prepared to do your own mahi/work on this journey. We live in a rich tapestry of the many cultures that now form our communities, each having their own unique celebrations. Each thread has its own beauty and woven alongside each other, they can form an amazing expression of what it means to be human. Treat everything that is shared with you as a gift.

NOTES ABOUT THE USE OF STORYTELLING, DANCE AND DRAMA

At the heart of this resource is storytelling. There are so many things I could say about storytelling and stories, but in short, I encourage you to remember these few things.

Stories are perhaps the dominant way of how we make sense of what happens to us and around us. They are "the map and not the territory." However, perhaps this expression does not fully express the complex and nuanced relationship between these two ideas. Mythologies, which form the greater part of the body of traditional stories, are deeply symbolic and may be both esoteric in nature and engaging with a 'beyond rational' way of making sense of the world. Stories are not benign. They are human constructions and carry with them all the messy, wonderful and sometimes painful complexities of being human. You can think of them as the largest invisible organising system in this world.

For a very long time stories were, (and in some places continue to be), experiences that were shared orally. This meant we were always in a relationship with at least one other person when we shared stories, usually more. Technology, in particular writing, has robbed us of the requirement of physical proximity to each other, which has a special very old 'magic' to it. It has also robbed us of context and with visual forms of storytelling, especially digital, our own agency of imagining. When children want us to share a story with them, it is not just the content of the story and the experience of entertainment that comes from sharing a story together, it is the desire for intimacy that is called for. In the words of Jack Maguire, *"telling a story is offering an expression of love."*

These days, many traditional stories (that have no individual authorship) come to us in the written form. Please remain aware of how these written sources have come into being:

• Who are the collectors/authors/editors and how might they have altered the story?

• What is the historic context in which stories may have been acquired or transcribed?

These are some of the qualifying questions I ask myself when telling stories from cultures other than my own:

1. **Is there someone else who could/should be telling this story? Would they be willing and how can I support them?**

2. **Am I giving this story the respect it deserves, taking the time to inform myself, get the pronunciation of names and places correct etc.**

3. **What is motivating me to share this story?**

4. **What is my relationship with this story and the culture it comes from? It's good to make these connections visible.**

5. **Do I stand to personally benefit from sharing this story? If so, how can I share that benefit with others.**

You will find in each season's chapter, stories that I have adapted for sharing from various cultures. Let these simply be a starting point in your storytelling journey. Find stories from your own whakapapa and ones that reflect the cultures of the tamariki you are working with. Share stories that ignite curiosity in you and have fun creating new stories. For more about stories and storytelling you might

want to read my earlier publication, *The Story Sack: Storytelling and Story Making with Young Children.*

DANCES AND DRAMA

Dance and drama are other age-old means of sharing and exploring stories. However, while all drama is a form of storytelling, not all dances are narratives. There is a simple joy in being embodied and moving in ways that predates the evolution of language.

The drama episodes I share are informed by the theory of 'drama in education' or 'process drama,' pioneered by the English educator Dorothy Heathcote. I feel the best way to think about process drama for young children, is as the thoughtful complication of children's own imaginative play. Instead of listening to a story, we become the story, making decisions that shape the story. There is no separate audience. Those participating in the drama are both the agents and the spectators. I have included in the appendix an introduction to process drama from my book, *'Imagined Worlds: A Journey Through the Expressive Arts in Early Childhood.'*

The first language of children is movement. My approach to dance and movement draws upon the work of Rudolf Laban, an Austro- Hungarian dancer and educator who created the framework for the conceptual approach to teaching dance.

Again, for more information about this kaupapa you can read my book, *'Dance Upon a Time - Dances of the Feet and Tongue.'*

ON QUESTIONING

One of the crucial things I have learnt as a teacher, is the importance of the quality of our questioning. In my mind, curiosity is the basis of life-long learning and we need to feed that fire in our children.

There are many different types of questions and we need to be mindful of how we use them. Imagine that questions are like keys, each one leading us through a different door. We don't want to be going into the same room all the time when there is a universe to explore.

Children can quickly learn from our use of questioning, that a question is an opportunity to guess what the adult is thinking or obtain a 'right' answer. We are usually praised when we're judged to have responded in a way that is 'right'. We all like to be praised and so fall into the habit of trying to 'get it right' rather than to understand.

One way to break this habit is to change our use of language.

Rather than saying:

"Where does fire come from?"

We could say,

"I wonder where fire comes from?"

The simple addition of those two words, 'I wonder', shifts the relationship from that of the expert asking the novice, to an invitation to curiously investigate the idea together as co-collaborators.

'To wonder' is to be in a place of awe. The experience of awe is important in unlocking our receptiveness to a profound sense of significance and connection.

THE VALUE OF CELEBRATING THE SEASONS

Once, when more of us were actively involved with growing/foraging/hunting our food, our lives were more closely entwined with the changing seasons. Not surprisingly, many major human celebrations were seasonally relevant. We paid attention to what was happening around us because our well-being depended on it. Which berry was available when, which animals migrated and returned at what time of year, which winds blew when for navigation and travel. As climate changes and extreme weather events increase, we are learning the hard way that our lives still do depend on what's happening in our environment.

When we collectively and consciously celebrate the seasons we build connection and affection for our immediate surroundings and for each other. When we pay attention to the trees that grow with us, we are more likely to protect them. When we regularly visit our local waterways – the ocean, river, lakes, wetlands or streams, we observe seasonal changes, develop relationships, notice adverse changes and are more likely to be active caretakers and advocates. We are more likely to see ourselves as part of an environment rather than separate from it.

The changing of seasons is an amplification of our own smaller lives. The natural human lifespan can be viewed as changing seasons – spring being

our birth and early years, summer our young adult lives, autumn our middle age and winter, old age and death. We can also see in the natural world our own experiences – the vigour and excitement of spring in a new idea or project, summer as a time of exploration and activity, autumn as the time to reap a 'harvest' from our efforts and winter as the natural conclusion to a project or relationship. Some of the most profound teachings can come from the natural world – that light and

darkness both have their place, that rest should be an important part of our lives, that change is inevitable, that the fruits of our actions bear the seeds for future life and that every season has its gifts.

CULTIVATING AN AWARENESS OF THE SEASONS

When people gather together to celebrate, there are some fundamentals that remain constant across these festivities. We share food, stories, sing, dance and often exchange gifts.

These activities were all initially informed through observation and a relationship with the lived environment. So let's begin by returning to the basics of celebration and tune into what is happening in our immediate surroundings.

Many of us now live in urban environments with either restricted or little access to 'green spaces' and in homes that are air conditioned and illuminated by artificial light. We move around in little boxes on wheels that separate us from the landscape we travel through, and are informed by screens that offer us windows into every corner of our planet. We eat food from the supermarket that is sourced from all over the world and take walks plugged into our own personal soundtracks. In short, while technology has afforded us 'the world

at our fingertips' we're often disconnected from what is actually happening in our own proverbial 'back yard'.

So how about beginning with a walk to connect with what's happening out there in our immediate environment? Let's take our feet out to kiss the earth that your community calls home (kick off those shoes on the days and in the places you can). You may have a park, a water way or some bush nearby you can visit. If not, maybe you have a playground area that you can explore with new eyes.

Here's a simple activity you can begin with. You might want to play it during or at the end of your walk.

SENSING THE SEASON

Talking to our tamariki about their own observations and understandings is always a good place to begin any exploration. The simple game 'I spy with my little eye' can be adapted to extend beyond the visual to encompass some of our other senses. The 'I spy' can also shift to the 'we spy'. Sometimes the collective and the individual can experience the world differently.

I/we spy with my/our little eye/s, something that looks like (spring, summer, autumn, winter)

I/we hear with my/our little ear/s, something that sounds like (spring, summer, autumn, winter)

I/we sniff with my/our little nose/s, something that smells like (spring, summer, autumn, winter)

I/we taste with my/our little tongue/s, something that grows in (spring, summer, autumn, winter)

The more often you make time in your routine to draw attention to what is happening around you, the more observant you will become. We can choose where we place our attention.

If you are going to make these walks a regular part of your routine I suggest returning to specific areas or trees so that there is a consistency of relationship which enables you to observe change over time. With the technology many of us carry around in our pockets these days, it's easy to photograph trees, a field or waterways at different times of the year. However, I urge you to not let technology become the dominating eye in this exercise – just a tool for recording. Keep your focus on using your own senses.

AN INVITATION TO LAY THE TABLE FOR THE SEASON

Just as we would set a place at our table for a guest, we can create a designated place in our space to celebrate and acknowledge the passing season. This could be a table or box, an area on the wall, a mat, a shelf or you could even create a seasonal shrine outdoors.

Encourage the children to collect/bring objects that signify the season to place in this created space. At the beginning of each season's chapter I'll make suggestions to give you some ideas but there will be regional differences and I encourage you to investigate what's pono/true for you. Items could include flowers/plants, pictures of animals or activities, food that is seasonal, coloured fabric, symbols (e.g. eggs for spring), written words associated with the season etc. You can create a ritual to do this (gathering the group together in the area and singing a song), or make a casual contribution, or a combination of both. I suggest when you establish or transition the space, that you do something collectively. This will be part of your celebration.

SINGING THE SEASON

I love singing seasonal songs. Of course, we have this tradition with Christmas carols but we can sing songs for every season. I will be sharing some songs I have created or enjoy but strongly encourage you to source songs from your own communities or make a song up together. Making up a song is so much fun and it will be uniquely yours. You do not have to be a musical genius to do this. We are all born with an instrument, our voice, and we already know lots of songs. So here is an easy way to make up a seasonal song.

1. **Use a tune everyone is familiar with e.g. (Twinkle Little Star, Frère Jacques)**

2. **Collect ideas together with the children about the season – this can naturally lead on from your walk and or sensory game**

3. **Make up as many verses as you like**

4. **Add actions to your song (this will always help you remember the words)**

Example to the tune of Frère Jacques

SUMMER SONG

It is sunny, it is sunny
The days are long, the days are long
We like going swimming, we like
                    going swimming
Because it's hot, because it's hot

We eat strawberries, we eat strawberries
And peaches too, and peaches too
We need to wear our hats outside
We need to wear our hats outside
Or else we'll get burnt, or else we'll get
                    burnt

Example to the tune of Twinkle, Twinkle Little Star

WINTER SONG

Winter, winter you are cold
On the mountain there is snow
We light fires to keep us warm
Days are short and nights are long
Winter, hats and gloves are on
I see my breath as I sing this song

EATING THE SEASON

If you have fruit/food sharing as part of your routine, make it local and seasonal (and organic - or at the very least spray free whenever possible). It will be more cost effective. Seasonal foods often contain what our bodies need for developing immunity to seasonal bugs and it is a great way to create conversation and connection about the season and what is growing. This can also be done with herbal teas, which I have found many children enjoy.

Note: if you are ever unsure about whether a plant is safe to eat/drink, seek advice before consuming/sharing it.

MEASURING THE SEASON

You might like to consider investing in a rain gauge, thermometer or weather station for your group. Measuring and charting changes in rainfall and temperature can be a great visual record of seasonal change and brings a scientific perspective to the experience.

SUMMER - RAUMATI

Te tātarakihi, te pihareinga; ko ngā manu ēnā o Rehua.

Māori Whakataukī

The cicada and the cricket are the songbirds of summer.

Māori Proverb

Summertime and the livin' is easy.

DuBose Heyward

In te ao Māori, raumati means the time of one hundred hands because if you were/are growing food it's the busiest time in the māra/garden. Plants need tending, watering, mulching, protecting and weeding. Traditionally summer is when you grow the food that will be preserved and stored to eat over the leaner months of winter and early spring.

These are the days of light and warmth that energise us. They have become our time of holidays, festive celebrations, New Year and days on the beach. Our seasonal feasts embrace the summer foods of salads, kai moana and pavlova while still enjoying the inherited northern winter foods of mince pies and fruitcake.

Because of the overlay of the northern winter festivals during the southern summer we end up having everything at once - festive celebrations, holidays, summer solstice, Christmas and New Year - it can be quite exhausting! We are trying to rest and start a new cycle in the middle of a seasonal high. No wonder we often end up feeling a bit frazzled!

LAYING THE TABLE FOR SUMMER

I wonder what the qualities of summer are?
Suggestions: Warmth, light, busyness, heat, being outdoors

I wonder which plants we usually see in summer?
Suggestions: pōhutukawa, sunflowers, rata, mānuka, cabbage tree/ tī kōuka

I wonder which foods we have available to eat in summer?
Suggestions: strawberries, stone fruits (peaches, plums, nectarines), blueberries, zucchini, cucumbers, new potatoes, kawakawa fruit, watercress

I wonder which animals we see in summer?
Suggestions: Bees, bumble bees, frogs, butterflies, fledglings, dolphins (any ocean dwelling creatures), cicadas, flies

I wonder who the atua/deities that can be associated with summer are?
Suggestions: Tāma-nui-te-rā, Apollo, Sol, Áine, Amaterasu

A FOOT STORY

THE TWO GECKOS WHO WENT TO THE SEA

Please see notes in the appendix on foot stories. (P 126)

Once upon a time there were two geckos, and when this story started they were fast asleep, snoring. **Legs stretched out straight in front of the body, toes pointing down to the floor and flexing back towards the chest to the rhythm of the snores.**

When one little gecko woke up and said, "Hooray, what shall we do today." **Lift your right leg and shake.**

He tried to wake up his friend, "Wake up! Wake up!" **Tap left leg with right leg.**

But his friend was fast asleep, so the little gecko went and fetched an alarm clock. **Left leg continues to point and flex. Right leg bends and tip toes out to the side, level with the hip and returns to front centre. Both legs stretched out straight in front of the body.**

The alarm clock went, "Brrrrrrring," but the little gecko still slept. **Shake the whole body gently.**

So the alarm clock rang louder, "Brrrrring," but still the gecko slept. **Shake the whole body a little more vigorously.**

So the alarm clock rang as loud as it could, "Brrrrring." **Shake the whole body with force.**

And the little gecko jumped up, "Hooray!" **Lift your left foot into the air and return to the floor.**

"Hooray!" said her friend. "What shall we do today?"

Turn feet towards each other, and wriggle each foot in turn as it speaks.

"It's summer, let's go to the beach."

"But first, let's do our exercises."

So the two little geckos went point and flex and point and flex. **Point and flex feet.**

Round and around and around and around and then the other way. **Ankle rotations (turn feet in small circles from the ankle) of both feet in both directions.**

Then in and out, and in and out, and in and out. **In a sitting position jump feet apart and then back together again three times.**

And then off they set. They went walk, walk, walk, walk. Skippity-hop, skippity-hop, jump, jump, jump, jump. Stop! (x2) **Rhythm of different steps performed using the feet in a sitting position, with bent knees.**

The beach was big and white and sandy. The sea was wide and blue and deep. It was the biggest thing that those two geckos had ever seen. They ran as fast as they could along the sand jumping over the pieces of driftwood. **Using your feet, keep the rhythm of a run on the floor on the spot. Keep your knees bent and lift your right leg and move it in an arc to the right of centre. Return to the floor. Left foot follows. (Repeat three time on each side)**

When they couldn't run anymore they started to dig a sandcastle. **Stretching forward towards the feet with alternate arms as if reaching for something. Stretches should move progressively upwards until the arms reach above the head.**

They built it as high as they could and then they knocked it to the ground and built another. **Shake the upper body and arms down towards the feet.** (Repeat sequence 3 times)

"Look over there!" squeaked one of the geckos. Resting on the beach was a rowboat. The two geckos scampered over and put on the life jackets, zipping them up. **Sitting in an upright position with knees bent. As the zipper is fastened, straighten your back and move your shoulders backwards.**

Then taking hold of the oars they started to row:

Row, row, row your boat

Reach forwards towards your feet with your arms as if rowing. As you pull back, engage the stomach muscles.

Gently over the sea

Raise arms alternately out to the side in a side stretch over the head.

If you see a great big shark

Open legs wide into a scissor stretch, then snap shut.

Don't forget to scream!

Springing arms and legs open.

The little geckos didn't see any sharks but they did find two fishing lines in the boat. They cast out their lines and waited for a bite. SNAP! **From an upright sitting position with bent knees, open legs out again into a scissor stretch. Arms stretch down towards feet, keeping legs straight and 'SNAP' on toes.**

Slowly, slowly they pulled in their lines and there was a great wobbling jellyfish, who went wobble, wobble, wobble. **Creep fingers back up legs. Shake upper body and arms to the rhythm of wobble, wobble, wobble.**

So they cast out their lines and waited for a bite. SNAP! **From an upright sitting position with bent knees, open legs out again into a scissor stretch. Arms stretch down towards feet, keeping legs straight and 'SNAP' on toes.**

They slowly, slowly pulled in their lines and there was a stingray, who went flap, flap, flap. **Creep fingers back up legs. Bring soles of your feet together with bent knees, making a diamond shape with your legs. Gently pulse your legs to the rhythm of flap, flap, flap.**

So they cast out their lines for the last time and waited for a bite. SNAP! **From an upright sitting position with bent knees, open legs out again into a scissor stretch. Arms stretch down towards feet, keeping legs straight and 'SNAP' on toes.**

They pulled in their lines and there was a big clump of floppy seaweed that went flippity, floppity, flippity, floppity. **Creep fingers back up legs. Release spine and allow body to fall and gently pulse over left leg and then right leg to the rhythm of flippity, floppity.**

Suddenly the waves began to grow larger. The boat rocked this way. The boat rocked that way. The boat rocked forwards and the boat rocked backwards and it nearly tipped over. But it didn't. **Extend your right arm out on your right hand side, pressing hand to floor as your left arm stretches up and over the head, lengthening the left hand side of the body. Repeat on the left hand side of the body. Crossing legs, stretch forwards towards the floor with both arms. With knees bent, lift feet off the floor, and lean backwards. Moving into a balance, engage the stomach muscles. Hold and relax.**

The two geckos rowed back home:

Row, row, row your boat
Reach forwards towards your feet with your arms as if rowing. As you pull back, engage the stomach muscles.
Gently over the sea
Raise arms alternately out to the side in a side stretch over the head.
If you see a great big shark
Open legs wide into a scissor stretch, then snap shut.
Don't forget to scream!
Springing arms and legs open.

Back on the dry sand they went walk, walk, walk, walk. Skippity-hop, skippity-hop, jump, jump, jump, jump. Stop! (x2)
Rhythm of different steps performed using the feet in a sitting position, with bent knees.

And when they reached home, they jumped into bed and it wasn't long before you could hear them snoring.
Lower legs to ground as upper body lifts from the floor into an upright position; legs resting straight on the floor in front of the body as toes point and flex to the rhythm of snoring.

FUN WITH THE SUN

Recording available ♪

The sun is at its zenith during summer. In December we have the summer solstice, the longest day of the year. It's no coincidence that Christmas falls a few days after the solstice. Christian Festivals were often overlaid onto existing seasonal festivals. The sun has always been a popular deity throughout the world; this is not surprising as its warmth and light are the source of life on our planet. As much as we love the sun, we have learnt to be cautious of it over time and a sunhat is an essential part of our summer attire.

In te ao Māori, Tamanui-te-rā (the sun) has two wives. His summer wife is Hine Raumati and his winter wife Hine Takurua. Tamanui-te-rā spends his time traveling between his two wives/ punarua. The whare/house of Hine Raumati is on Earth. When Tamanui-te-rā or Te Rā is with Hine Raumati, we experience warmer weather. Summer solstice, the longest day of the year, is the day Te Rā leaves his summer wife and begins his journey back to his winter wife, Hine Takurua.

The whare/house of Hine Takurua is away from Earth over the ocean. When Te Rā is with Hine Takurua, we experience the cooler weather. Winter solstice, the shortest day of the year, is the day Te Rā leaves his winter wife and begins his journey back to his summer wife, Hine Raumati. The longest day in the Southern Hemisphere will always be the shortest day in the Northern Hemisphere and vice versa.

Activity

Divide the room in half. On the far side of the room is the home of Hine Raumati (summer). On the opposite side of the room is the whare of Hine Takurua (winter). Discuss the different activities that humans do in summer and winter:

"During raumati, we swim, go to the beach, barbeque, work in the garden, etc."

"During takurua, we play in the snow, rest, sit by the fire, etc."

As the music changes, the group moves between the two whare/sides of the room and dance the actions of the activities of the different seasons as narrated.

SALLY GO ROUND THE SUN

a traditional European song and circle dance

Part A.

Sally (*this of course can be changed out for a child's name*) **goes round the sun**
Sally goes round the moon
Sally goes round the chimney pot every (*or whatever day it is*) **afternoon**

Part B.

The sun goes up, the sun goes down
The sun goes spinning round and round

(The tune for Part A is 'the Farmer in the Dell – I've created part B as an add on that can just be chanted)

This can be shared in a number of different ways.

1. **Make a standing circle together. Choose one/two children to dance around the outside of the circle while part A. is being sung. Before singing part B, they rejoin the circle, and everyone performs the actions of part B together.**

2. **Make a standing circle together. Choose a child to be the sun and a child to be the moon. They stand in the centre of the circle. Explain that everyone else will be a chimney pot (you might need to explain what a chimney pot is!). The chosen child whose name you sing, then dances around the sun and moon and then around all the other children who are chimney pots. With older children they can weave in and out of the chimney pots. Before singing part B, they rejoin the circle and everyone performs the actions of part B together.**

3. **Make a standing circle together holding hands. As you sing, move in one direction singing part A. Stop and let go of each other's hands, sing part B, and then change directions.**

4. **If you want to get really clever with older children, you can make two circles – one sitting inside the other. Part A of the song can be sung in a round. One circle goes in one direction and the other circle goes in the other direction. They stop and perform Part B together.**

I bet you can even find other ways to share this old favourite. It can be used for learning days of the week or thinking of interesting ways that Sally travelled around the sun (in a rocket, on a bird, on a star, on a magic carpet etc).

There are many stories about the sun. The best known story in Aotearoa is the story of Māui and how he slowed the sun. I learnt the Chinese story of the ten suns when I was working as a storyteller at the Auckland Museum, a regular annual event. I was asked to tell a story during the Chinese New Year, which always falls during the southern summer.

THE STORY OF THE TEN SUNS
(Chinese mythology)

Recording available

Long ago when the world was still new, there was not just the one sun that we know today but ten suns. Each day the ten suns would travel with their mother, the goddess Xi He, to the Valley of the Light in the East. There in the great lake, Xi He would wash her children and hang them in the branches of an enormous mulberry tree called Fu-sang. Then one at a time the suns would move off the tree into the sky and journey back to reach Mount Yen-Tzu in the Far West. One day the ten suns grew tired of this routine and they decided to all travel together across the sky. The heat of the ten suns in the sky made life on the Earth unbearable. Di Jun, the father of the ten suns, tried to persuade his children to appear only one at a time. But they would not listen to him. Di Jun called for the heavenly archer, Yi, armed with a magic bow and his quiver of ten arrows to frighten the disobedient suns. But the suns were defiant and Yi was forced to shoot nine of the suns, leaving only the one sun that we see today in the sky.

THE STORY OF THE TEN SUNS – AN ADAPTATION OF A TRADITIONAL CHINESE STORY

When I share this story with children, I often introduce it with a discussion about the sun. I wonder how many suns we have in our solar system? I wonder how far away the sun is? Interestingly this story came from the ten-day week the Chinese used to have. It's so easy to get locked into the idea that the reality that we occupy (the seven day week) is the only one. Stories are an effective way to introduce other possible realities. It's also a great story for counting, with lots of opportunities to add and subtract.

A quick beginning

Way, way, way back when the world was brand spanking new, there was not just one sun – there were…

Limited number of characters

One little, two little, three little suns, four little, five little, six little suns,
   Seven little, eight little, nine little suns, ten little suns in the sky. Hooray!

   (I sometimes tell a version with only five suns)

Straight-forward action

Every day the suns' mother would take them to the Great Eastern Lake. On the banks of the great eastern lake grew a mulberry tree that was guarded by the heavenly archer Yi. The suns would happily swim beneath the tree in the water while Yi watched.

Opportunities to participate

They would swim fast, and swim slow, swim up high and swim down low (children perform actions x 3). Then taking turns they would climb the great tree (up, up, up, up). They would give a BIG jump into the sky (wheeeee). And shine all the way across the sky until they reached the Western

Mountains, where they would jump down and rest. (Sing refrain for each sun's journey)

**Twinkle, twinkle, little sun,
shining bright on everyone**

Definite climax

But one day as the suns were swimming beneath the tree, they began to argue about who should go first.

"I'm always last," said sun number ten.

"Yeah, it's not fair, sun number one always gets to go first," said sun number five.

Repetitive patterns

So when it came time for sun number one to climb the tree, sun number five pushed ahead. He climbed up the great tree (up, up, up, up). And jumped into the sky (wheeeee).

Sun number one followed him. Up the great tree (up, up, up, up). And into the sky (wheeeee).

And they began to argue again. Now how many suns were there in the sky? Two suns arguing in the sky.

Sun number ten decided he should go up and try to stop the arguing. He climbed up the great tree (up, up, up, up). And into the sky (wheeeee). When the other seven suns saw suns one, five and ten in the sky, they thought it was a sun-fun free-for-all. So they all climbed up the great tree (up, up, up, up). And they all jumped into the sky (wheeeee). Ten suns shining in the sky.

More opportunities to participate

Now can you imagine how hot it was with ten suns in the sky? I wonder what was happening to everything down on earth? (Work with the children's suggestions – too hot, things were melting, burning up, fire, thirsty, sunburnt.) All the water on the earth dried up.

The people called out, "Oh it's so hot" (the rest of the group copies).

The animals called out, "Oh we are so thirsty" (the rest of the group copies).

The ten suns' mother and father called to their children, "Suns please come down" (the rest of the group copies).

But the suns were full of mischief and they would not listen. They answered, "Nah, nah, nah, nah, nah. We're so hot, we won't stop." (Children playing the roles of the sun copy)

Yi the heavenly archer, who stood beneath the great mulberry tree, saw that soon all the people and the animals, plants and insects would die. He too called to the suns, "Suns please come down" (the rest of the group copies).

But the suns just laughed and said, "Nah, nah, nah, nah, nah. We're so hot, we won't stop"(Children playing the roles of the sun copy).

And so Yi took one of his arrows and placed it in his bow. He pulled back the string...

And can you guess what he's going to do? Yes, he fired the arrow at sun number one, who fell down from the sky. (This part of the story can be sung and acted out using the tune Ten Green Bottles.)

There were ten shining suns hanging
in the sky
Ten shining suns hanging in the sky
Then Yi, fired an arrow
And one sun did die
Now there's only nine shining suns hanging
in the sky

Yi was about to shoot down the tenth sun, when all the people on earth called out, "Stop!" (the rest of the group copies). "Don't shoot down all the suns Yi. Please leave us one sun. Otherwise it will always be dark and cold and nothing will grow."

Satisfying conclusion

And so Yi left the tenth sun shining in the sky, which is the very sun that we have today.

Role-playing in storytelling

The Ten Suns story is great for getting children to take on roles. I would suggest first sharing the story as a told story, allowing the children to simply sit, listen and imagine. A second telling can then involve the children taking on roles. When asking children to be involved with acting out a story, you need to be clear about what decisions are yours and what choices the children can make, otherwise very quickly things can become chaotic. Storytelling isn't a play, so it's not necessary for every part of the story to be acted out. It can however be an effective means of engaging children.

Ten children can be selected to take on the parts of the ten suns. If there are more than ten children who would like to take part, explain that the story can be repeated another time/day and that even if they are not a sun this time you will need their help to tell the story. If you do not have ten suns, work with the number of suns you have! Each of the ten suns can be given a yellow ribbon/scarf, crepe paper, which can also work to signify whose turn it is. Ask the 'suns' to come

and stand near you, forming a long line facing the other children. As you tell the story, encourage the children to animate the actions of the suns by doing the actions with them – climbing the tree, jumping out into the sky, shining etc. When the children are not taking their turn encourage them to sit down. If you would really like to elaborate on this story, you can organise to have pieces of music – played, sung, recorded for each of the suns, when it is their turn to shine from the Eastern Lake to the Western Mountain. Each of the ten suns then has a chance to do a 'sun dance'.

In my experience, the children's favourite part of this story is when the suns get shot down! Understandably, you may prefer not to have anyone 'shot'. In some versions of this myth the suns are shot and are changed into birds as they fall to the earth. My personal favourite is to replace Yi's bow/arrow with a water pistol or a hose and to have him squirt them down. A story can be retold with many different endings. The original story can be told and then other possible endings discussed and shared.

Conclusion

Sharing songs, dances and stories about the sun is a good time to reinforce sun safe messages – wearing a hat, covering up, drinking water and staying out of the sun during the hottest times of the day. Here's a song that comes from Sun Safe Central that uses the tune of 'Row, Row, Row Your Boat' that I've used to make a sun hat game. Ask the children to get their hats/pōtae and sing the song and find fun places to wear your hats on different part of your body (shoulder, knee, back etc.)

**Sun, sun, sun is fun
When I wear my hat!
It helps protect my face and eyes
I put mine on like that!**

Choose a body part that's not your head to place your hat

You can play this with a leader that everyone copies or everyone can find their own way of wearing their hat. Conclude by wearing your hat on your head and reminding the tamariki about being 'sun-smart/safe'.

SUMMER ON THE BEACH

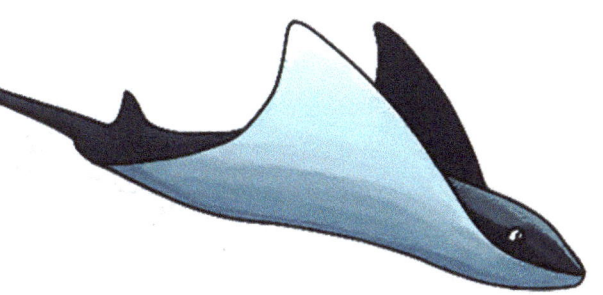

For those who live near a coastline (and in Aotearoa, the moana is never far away), the beach is the landscape of summer. Celebrating our coastlines and the creatures who live in the ocean is a fun way to encapsulate the qualities of summer and promote care of the moana.

Using the foot story of the two geckos who went to the beach or another ocean related story, encourage the children to share their own experience of visiting the beach.

- **I wonder how you got to the beach?**
- **I wonder what sorts of things you like to do at the beach?**
- **I wonder what sorts of things/animals you might see at the beach?**

These ideas can be worked into an action chant where as a group you can move the ideas suggested.

I (walked) to the beach
And what did I see?
A (seagull) who was looking at me
I (biked) to the beach

And what did I do?
Swim, swim
You can swim too

For those of you in Aotearoa here is a simple action song that explores some of the creatures who live in the moana/ocean using English and te reo Māori.

CREATURES OF THE MOANA

Mangō/mako – shark
Ika - fish
Tio - oyster
Wheke - octopus
Tepetepe -Jellyfish
Tohorā – whale
Pāpaka – crab
Kaukau – to swim

MAKO, MAKO I ROTO TE MOANA

Recording available ♪

Take turns at making the actions for each of the sea creatures as you move and sing, snapping hands or arms for a shark, swishing of the hips for a fish, wriggling arms for a wheke, wobbling the body for a jellyfish etc.

> Mako, mako
> I roto te moana
> Mako, mako
> In the sea (x2)
>
> Kaukau, kaukau
> Kaukau, kaukau
> You can swim along with me
> Kaukau, kaukau
> Kaukau, kaukau
> Swimming in the big blue sea

Recording available ♪

You will need a shell, preferably one that you can 'listen' to for this activity.

> Little shell, little shell
> Tell me about the ocean
> Little shell, little shell
> Tell me about the sea
> Where do you come from
> And where is your home
> Little shell, little shell
> That the waves sent to me

Ask the children to sit in a circle. As the song is sung the shell is passed around the circle. When the song finishes the person with the shell puts their ear to the shell and listens to a message from the sea. They may or may not want to relay this message to the group.

FESTIVE FOODS

Sharing food is central to most of our celebrations. Here are a few festive food ideas for the season. I've made the gingerbread character the traditional male character but this can be changed, as can the recipe. Why not have pizza dough, rēwena bread, focaccia, chapati, naan, tortilla or damper man!

THE KIWI GINGERBREAD MAN

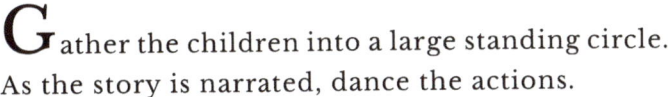

Recording available ♪

Gather the children into a large standing circle. As the story is narrated, dance the actions.

Once upon a time there was a little old lady. One day she decided to make some gingerbread men to share with her mokopuna/grandchildren when they came to stay for the holidays. So she got out her bowl **stretch arms to make a bowl shape** and she got out a spoon. **wave the spoon around the room** Now, a bowl is just a hole when it's got nothing in it – so she added the ingredients.

She shook in the flour. **shake the arms**

She punched in the butter. **forward punching action with arms**

She flicked in the ginger. **flick feet/hands**

She twisted in some sugar. **twist hips**

She rolled in the milk. **roll head**

combine ingredients, suggested with a stationary movement and a body part, repeat each movement three times

And then she stirred. She stirred with her hips. She stirred with her head. She stirred with her shoulders. She stirred with her arms. She stirred with her whole body. **stirring with different body parts**

Then she took that dough, and she rolled it this way, and she rolled it that way. **either sit on the floor with legs stretched in front of the body and roll the body to the right and then to the left or stay standing and roll with the arms or turn the whole body to the right and then to the left**

She gave him raisins for eyes, and a raisin for his nose, and raisins that buttoned right down to his toes. **touching different parts of the body as they are spoken, reaching right down to toes**

Then she put the gingerbread man into the oven. **sit on the floor with legs stretched forward, feet pointing into the centre of the circle** The oven was hot and as the gingerbread man cooked he rose, up, up, up, up. **rest palms of hands on the floor just to the rear of the hips. Pushing down with the arms, lift the hips and legs off the floor, so that the weight of the body is supported by hands and heels**

The old woman opened the door, and the cold air made the dough sink. **lower hips and legs back to the floor** Not ready yet.

The oven was hot and as the gingerbread man cooked

he rose, up, up, up, up. **rest palms of hands on the floor just to the rear of the hips. Pushing down with the arms, lift the hips and legs off the floor, so that the weight of the body is supported by hands and heels** The old woman opened the door, and the cold air made the dough sink. **lower hips and legs back to the floor**

Not ready yet.

The oven was hot and as the gingerbread man cooked he rose, up, up, up, up. **rest palms of hands on the floor just to the rear of the hips. Pushing down with the arms, lift the hips and legs off the floor, so that the weight of the body is supported by hands and heels** The old woman opened the

door, and out jumped the gingerbread man **jump up off the floor and into a standing position**

He gave himself a shake **shake body** and said, "run, run as fast as you can, you can't catch me because I'm the gingerbread man." x 2 **running in self space/on the spot**

Out the door he ran. And he ran and he ran until he met a jumping green frog. **travelling through space with a run or on the spot**

The jumping green frog called: "STOP, gingerbread man STOP!" **running stops. Encourage children to repeat this refrain with you**

But the gingerbread man did not. He said: "Jump, jump as fast as you can, you can't catch me I'm the gingerbread man" x 2 **locomotive movement changes to jump**

So the frog jumped, and the gingerbread man ran. And he ran and he ran and he ran until he came to a hopping white rabbit.

The hopping white rabbit called: "STOP, gingerbread man STOP!" **running stops. Encourage children to repeat this refrain with you**

But the gingerbread man did not. He said: "Hop, hop as fast as you can, you can't catch me I'm the gingerbread man" x 2 **Locomotive movement changes to hop**

Repeat sequence for as many hungry animals as you choose:

Lamb – skip
Horse – gallop
Snake – slide
Bird – flap
Alien – wobble
Kererū – flap
Fish/whale – swim

And so the bird flapped, the snake slid, the horse galloped, the rabbit hopped, the frog jumped and the gingerbread man ran. He ran and he ran and he ran until he came to a river. The river was deep and the river was wide and there was no bridge to the other side, and deep down in that river there lived a big hungry eel/tuna, or if in Australia, a crocodile. **sitting down on floor with legs stretched out in front of the body**

The eel said to the gingerbread man: "I will carry you across the river. Climb onto my tail" **sitting on the floor, children touch each body part is mentioned and gently pat it**

On jumped the gingerbread man and out into the river the eel swam.

"The river is deep and the river is fast," said the eel. "Climb a little higher onto my back."

And the gingerbread man did.

"The river is cold and the river is dangerous", said the eel. "Climb onto my head."

And the gingerbread man did.

"The river is wide and the river is rough," said the eel. "Climb onto my nose."

And the gingerbread man did.

And the eel opened his mouth wide, and wider and wider and went SNAP. **open legs and arms wide into a scissor stretch and then SNAP closed** And that was the end of the gingerbread man.

Notes:

With young children it is best to keep a single focus and encourage the children to dance all the different locomotor movements together. The characters/animals that the gingerbread man meets and their movements can be changed as the children think of different ideas and forms of locomotion. It's great to use animals that are familiar to your locale and native birds/mammals/reptiles and fish. Encourage children to 'unpack' the movement potential in the animals/characters that they suggest.

Older children might want to break the story into parts and take responsibility for the different characters and their movements. This movement story is very high energy. It should be called the 'aerobic-bread man,' so it is a welcome relief to reach the 'river', sit down and gently stretch for both the dancing children and adults. However the whole story can be danced 'upright' if need be. The speed measurement of fast can be varied to add different challenges:

- **Skip as high as you can.**
- **Slide as low as you can.**
- **Jump as big as you can.**

MAKING A FRUIT SALAD

Recording available

This is another food focused movement activity. Discuss with the children their favourite summer fruits. You may even wish to bring along a kete/basket of in-season fruit and use this as a starting place for thinking about favourite fruits.

You can use the chant:

What have I got in the basket?
What have I got in the basket?
What have I got in the basket?
At (kindy/school/playcentre etc) today

He aha kei roto i te kete?
He aha kei roto i te kete?
He aha kei roto i te kete?
I tēnei rā

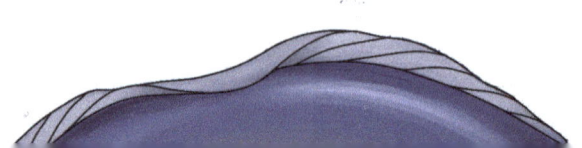

If not using real fruit you might also consider using pictures of fruit. Ask children what are some of their favourite summer fruits. Establish that you have a big imaginative bowl in the centre of the circle and that, as a group we are going to make fruit salad in it. With each fruit suggested, perform the chopping of the fruit. You can chop with your fingers, hands, arms, legs, head etc. Vary the chopping to fast, slow or high or low chopping.

You could use a rhyme like:

**Chop, chop, chop
Into the pot
Every little bit, makes for a lot
Chop, chop, chop
Into the pot
We give thanks for what we've got**

OR

**Chippity chop, chippity chop — we're making fruit salad in the big pot
Chippity chair, chippity chair — when it's all made, fruit salad we'll share**

When fruit suggestions have been exhausted, give the salad a 'movement stir' with different body parts: Stir with your knees, stir with your shoulders. Once the fruit salad has been stirred, everyone can take an 'imaginative' bowl of fruit salad to eat. You may wish to follow up this movement activity by making a real fruit salad to eat.

A FESTIVE PLUM STORY

There is a wonderful northern winter festive tradition called wassailing, where people go and sing to their fruit trees (traditionally it was the apple trees) to encourage them to fruit well the following season. Perhaps you might consider wassailing your local fruit trees as part of your celebrations (though wassailing was traditionally done during winter when the trees are dormant).

I created this story a few years ago with the children of Awaawaroa Eco Village, where I live, for a community Christmas event. We have an early plum tree in the village that is always ready with fruit from mid to late December. The people who grew it kindly let us all come and pick early plums every year. So here is the story:

It was nearly the summer holidays and the plum tree was heaving. The branches hung heavy with delicious ripe juicy red plums. Everyone at (name of EC Centre/school/family) looked forward to the plums – they were the flavour of the season.

One afternoon (teacher/parent) and the children went to pick a basket of plums to share for the end of year party. But they couldn't believe their eyes when they reached the plum tree. The tree was bare. Not a single plum remained. Where have all the plums gone? they puzzled.

"All the plums off the plum tree have gone missing and there's none for the party this afternoon. Do you think you could try and work out where the plums have gone?"

"Sure!" said the children, "we'll solve the mystery."

The children looked around to see if they could find any clues.

"Hey look?" shouted (child's name), "I see something red in the long grass. It's a plum."

The children found a trail of plums leading down to the awa/river where the tuna/eel lived.

"Hey tuna," said the children, "have you taken the Christmas plums?"

The eel/tuna wriggled and swam and said:

Plums, plums
We like meat
Frogs and rats
Are our treats

"Urgh!" said the children.

And they continued following the trail of plums. When, who should they meet but some pūkeko.

"Hey pūkeko," said the children, "have you taken the plums?"

The pūkeko gave a squawk, flicked their tails and said:

Plums, plums
Plums are yum
But we have eaten only one
Or maybe two...

"Hmmm," said the children, looking suspicious.

But the pūkeko flew away and the trail of plums continued. When, who should they meet but some rabbits

"Hey rabbits," said the children, "have you taken the Christmas plums?"

The rabbits hopped and wriggled their noses and said:

Plums, plums
Are not our habit
They grow too high
For hungry rabbits

"Hey I see another one," shouted (child's name), "Follow me."

The trail of plums continued. When, who should they meet but some peacocks?

"Hey peacocks," said the children, "have you taken the plums?"

The peacocks crowed, spread their tails and said:

Plums, plums
Might be yummy
But leafy greens
Fill our tummy

"I wonder if we'll ever solve this mystery?" said (child's name).

The trail of plums continued down the road to where a family of pigs lived.

"Hey piggies," said the children, "have you taken the plums?"

The pigs grunted and said:

Plums, plums
What a treat
But we're fenced in
We're not the thieves

The children were growing tired. They had been searching all afternoon. But the trail of plums continued and headed towards the kindergarten/school etc. From the (school, ec centre, hall etc) came the sound of laughter, music and people talking.

The children followed the trail into the building. The end of the year party had started and there, on the table was a big bowl filled with red, juicy, delicious Christmas plums.

"I picked them this morning for the party," said (another teacher/adult) "for everyone to share."

The plum mystery was solved.

The children popped plums into their mouths and said:

Plum, plums
Delicious plums
There is enough for everyone

A MID-SUMMER OR A MID-WINTER CHRISTMAS?

I have given much thought as to where the celebration of Christmas should be placed in this resource. Christmas for Christians is the celebration of the birth of Jesus Christ. Even if you are not a practising Christian, Christianity's influence runs deep in Australia and New Zealand.

Yet, many of the traditions associated with Christmas predate the Christian celebration and are steeped in mid-winter European traditions. The traditional Christmas tree (a custom made popular by Queen Victoria) is a northern conifer, one of the few evergreen trees in midwinter, Father Christmas (an amalgamation of religious, folkloric and commercial stories) lives in the North Pole, and the tradition of decorating with lights/candles provided illumination in what was a very dark time of year.

In New Zealand, Matariki now rightfully occupies the place as our seasonal and indigenous mid-winter celebration, and winter solstice and mid winter Christmas celebrations are also becoming more common.

Of all our upside down seasonal celebrations, Christmas, over the last two hundred plus years, has slowly shifted to fit the character of the season. Antipodean depictions of Santa often have him pictured in red and white trimmed shorts and a t-shirt relaxing on the beach. Here in Aotearoa we now have Hana kōkō - the word in te reo Māori for Santa Claus. There are many childrens' picture books telling stories of a 'Kiwi' or 'Australian' Christmas.

In the northern regions of the country, our Christmas tree is the Pōhutukawa tree, but people often decorate any tree they like to be their Christmas tree. I'm a big fan of living native Christmas trees that can later be planted out (I'd suggest waiting until winter to plant them out though). I'm also a big fan of heirloom decorations (good quality reusable decorations), natural decorations – decorating with shells from the beach, pinecones etc., edible decorations – popcorn and biscuits and home-made paper decorations – paper chains, origami etc.

THE CHRISTMAS TREE

A SEASONAL
DANCE/MOVEMENT STORY

Recording available ♪

I wonder who has helped decorate a Christmas tree before? (Maybe you have one in your centre/ class room that you can refer to or a picture of one). I wonder what shapes and decorations you used to decorate the tree? Stars, baubles, angels/faeries, birds, popcorn, flashing lights, long paper chains etc.

Christmas Eve is a magical time when unusual things can happen. Can you go and find a place in the room and curl up under the Christmas tree to dance this magic Christmas Eve story? (you may wish to use place markers/mats to help locate the children in the room).

Twas the night before Christmas Day and everyone was very excited. The Christmas tree stood tall, beautifully decorated and everyone had gone to bed so that Santa Claus could visit. Mum/Dad/Nana/Kuia/Koro turned off the lights and in the darkness, magic started to happen. The Christmas decorations started to move. **children can stand to move or make shapes on the floor, encourage the children to make a shape with their bodies – as you narrate the story you can model the movements**

There were round homemade biscuits
twisting shells collected from the beach
Angels/faeries with outstretched wings
And long, stretched paper chains of bright colours that the children had made

When everyone was asleep they jumped off the Christmas tree and went dancing around the room. **children leave place makers or move from locomotor/non locomotor movement and dance around the room** You can give verbal provocations to challenge the quality of the movement. For example:

They danced up high
They danced backwards
They danced with another decoration/friend

But when Mum/Dad/Koro heard all the noise and came down and turned on the lights, all the Christmas decorations were back on the Christmas tree, still and silent. **the children freeze on the spot or return back to their space mat and make a shape** Mum/Dad/Koro turned off the light and went back to bed and the decorations started to come to life again.

There were flashing lights
And flapping birds
Angels blowing trumpets
And drummers drumming

And they all jumped off the Christmas tree and danced around the room. But when Mum/Dad/

Koro heard all the noise and came down and turned on the lights, all the Christmas decorations were back on the Christmas tree, still and silent. **the children freeze on the spot or return back to their space mat and make a shape** Mum/Dad/Koro turned off the light and went back to bed and the decorations started to come to life again.

There were pointed stars
And long popcorn chains
Little square parcels tied with a bow
And paper folded shapes that the children
                    had made themselves

And they all jumped off the Christmas tree and danced around the room. But when Mum/Dad/Koro heard all the noise and came down and turned on the lights, all the Christmas decorations were back on the Christmas tree, still and silent. **the children freeze on the spot or return back to their space mat and make a shape** Mum/Dad/Koro turned off the light and went back to bed and the decorations started to come to life and move again.

And then the decorations on the tree heard a sound on the roof: a clip, clip, clop, clip, clop of hooves and a "Ho, ho, ho." And so they stayed still and silent on the Christmas tree. I wonder what they saw? **encourage the children to share what they might have seen**

THE GIFT SONG

(an opportunity to practise
giving and receiving)

Recording available ♪

Gift exchange is a part of many seasonal celebrations. This gift giving song and activity shifts the focus from the material to the imaginative.

Here is a gift that we can all share
We pass it with love to all who are here
I wish you peace and happiness too
When I open this gift I'll share it with you

Sit with children on the floor in a circle. Sing this song as you pass a box around the circle. This needs to be a box of some description with an opening lid. Just like the game, 'pass the parcel', the box is passed around the circle while everyone sings the song. When the song ends, one of two things can happen:

1. The child who has the box, opens it and takes an imagined item/quality from the box (e.g a puppy, aroha/love etc)

2. The child who has the box when the song stops, chooses to give the box to someone else in the circle and then the chosen recipient opens the box and takes an imagined item/quality from the box (e.g a puppy, aroha/love etc)

Depending on the age of the children you can encourage the tamariki to:

1. Simply say what is the gift they have to share when they open the box

2. Mime what the gift is and encourage others to guess what it might be

3. Choose someone to give their gift to – this can be someone in the circle or someone not present (e.g "I want to give flowers to my Nana," Or "I want to give a turn of my bike to my brother.")

4. Encourage the recipient/s to respond to the experience of being given/receiving a gift

AUTUMN — NGAHURU

Ngahuru, kura kai, kura tangata

Māori Whakataukī

Harvest-time, wealth of food, the wealth of people

Māori proverb

At no other time (than autumn) does the earth let itself be inhaled in one smell, the ripe earth; in a smell that is in no way inferior to the smell of the sea, bitter where it borders on taste, and more honeysweet where you feel it touching the first sounds. Containing depth within itself, darkness, something of the grave almost.

Rainer Maria Rilke

In te ao Māori, autumn is commonly referred to as ngahuru which is an older word/kupu for the number ten (most of us are more familiar with tekau) – the tenth month of the maramataka, the lunar calendar.

Autumn is the time of harvest, a time of bounty, when everything offers up the fruits of the previous seasons' efforts – fruits, seeds and fully fledged young birds from the previous spring. Food is plentiful.

The autumn equinox, which falls in March, is the time of equal light and dark. The intense heat of summer has passed and many of the exotic trees of the northern hemisphere begin to turn. Everything is preparing for winter. Seed is produced ready for spring, some plants and animals become dormant and some migrate to warmer climates. Natural intelligence has a plan for winter.

LAYING THE TABLE FOR AUTUMN

I wonder what the qualities of autumn are?

Suggestions: Harvest, change, fruition

I wonder which plants we usually see in autumn?

Suggestions: Deciduous trees (liquid amber, oaks, maples), dahlias, chrysanthemums, many native plants/trees will have berries

I wonder which foods we have available to eat in autumn?

Suggestions: Pumpkins, kūmara, feijoas, apples, pears, hue, blackberries, coprosma berries, grapes, macadamias and other nuts

I wonder which animals we see in autumn?

Suggestions: Migrating birds and tuna/eels, rats and mice will be looking for warm winter homes

I wonder who the atua/deities that can be associated with autumn are?

Suggestions: Rongo-mā-tane, Pani, Persephone

AUTUMN SONG

a traditional English song

Recording available ♪

We have ploughed, we have sown
We have reaped and we have mown
We've bought home, all the load
Hip, hip, hip the harvest home

A FOOT STORY

TWO LITTLE GECKOS TAKE AN AUTUMN WALK

Please read the notes in the appendix about foot stories. (P 126)

Once upon a time there were two geckos and when this story started they were fast asleep, snoring. **Legs stretched out straight in front of the body, toes pointing down to the floor and flexing back towards the chest to the rhythm of the snores.**

When one little gecko woke up and said, "Hooray, what shall we do today." **Lift your right leg and shake.**

He tried to wake up his friend, "Wake up! Wake up!" **Tap left leg with right leg.**

But his friend was fast asleep, so the little gecko went and fetched an alarm clock. **Left leg continues to point and flex. Right leg bends and tip toes out to the side, level with the hip and returns to front centre. Both legs stretched out straight in front of the body.**

The alarm clock went, "Brrrrrrring." But the little gecko still slept. **Shake the whole body gently.**

So the alarm clock rang louder, "Brrrrring."

But still the gecko slept. **Shake the whole body a little more vigorously.**

So the alarm clock rang as loud as it could, "Brrrrring." **Shake your whole body with force.**

And the little gecko jumped up, "Hooray!" **Lift your left foot into the air and return to the floor.**

"Hooray!" said her friend. "What shall we do today?" **Turn feet towards each other, and wriggle each foot in turn as it speaks.**

"Let's go outside and play. **But first, let's do our exercises."**

So the two little geckos went point and flex and point and flex. **Point and flex feet.**

Round and around and around and around and then the other way. **Ankle rotations (turn feet in small circles from the ankle) of both feet in both directions.**

Then in and out and in and out and in and out. **In a sitting position jump feet apart and then back together again three times.**

And then off they set. They went walk, walk, walk, walk. Skippity-hop, skippity-hop, jump, jump, jump, jump. Stop! (x3) **Rhythm of different steps performed using the feet in a sitting position, with bent knees.**

In front of them was a big oak tree. **Stretch arms up over the head to make a tree shape with your body.**

And as they looked up they saw a bright red leaf fall, down, down, down to the ground. **Release one arm with a 'twisting' motion, float it 'leaf like'** back down towards the floor.

And then they saw a bright yellow leaf fall, down, down, down to the ground. **Release the other arm with a 'twisting' motion, float it 'leaf like' back down towards the floor.**

And then they saw more leaves fall, down, down, down to the ground. **Raise arms over the head and repeat action with both arms/wrists simultaneously.**

Soon under that big tree were great big piles of leaves. The little geckos scooped up the pile of leaves and threw them over their heads and shouted, "Whoopee!" **Open arms wide and then stretch down towards the feet, drawing the arms back towards the chest and throwing them up above the head shouting, "Whoopee!"** (repeat this three times).

Then they decided it would be fun to hide under the leaves. They buried themselves under the pile and waited, and waited, and waited... and leapt up shouting "whoopee!" **Curl your body up with your face down towards the floor (pose of the child) and the stretch up on '"whoopee!"** (x3)

When all of a sudden along came the wind and blew all the leaves away. **Roll arms in a circle shape.**

And so off they set. They went walk, walk, walk, walk. Skippity-hop, skippity-hop, jump, jump, jump, jump. Stop! (x3) **Rhythm of different steps performed using the feet in a sitting position, with bent knees.**

Until they reached the garden. In the garden

there were tall, tall broad beans. **Stretch arms upwards with straight backs.**

Carrots with feathery tops. **Hands open and wriggling on top of the head.**

Onions to make you cry, **Rub hands to eyes as if you were crying.**

And a fat round orange pumpkin. **Stretch arms in front and join to make a circle.**

"Let's make some vegetable soup," said the geckos.

So they picked, picked, picked the tall, tall broad beans. **Stretch arms upwards with straight backs.**

So they picked, picked, picked the carrots with feathery tops. **Hands open and wriggling on top of the head.**

So they picked, picked, picked the onions to make you cry, **Mock rubbing hands to eyes as if you were crying.**

And they picked, picked, picked the fat round orange pumpkin. **Stretch arms in front and join to make a circle.**

And taking them, they went walk, walk, walk, walk. Skippity-hop, skippity-hop, jump, jump, jump, jump. Stop! (x3) All the way home **Rhythm of different steps performed using the feet in a sitting position, with bent knees.**

At home they took the tall, tall broad beans and went, choppity, chop, choppity chop, choppity chop. Stop! **Repeat bean action, followed by a chopping motion with hands forward and then a**

hand stop signal with both hands.

Then they took the carrots with the feathery tops and went, choppity, chop, choppity chop, choppity chop. Stop! **Repeat carrot action, followed by a chopping motion with hands forward and then a hand stop signal with both hands.**

Then they took the onions that made you cry and went choppity, chop, choppity chop, choppity chop. Stop! **Repeat onion action, followed by a chopping motion with hands forward and then a hand stop signal with both hands.**

And finally they took the big fat pumpkin and went choppity, chop, choppity chop, choppity chop. Stop! **Repeat pumpkin action, followed by a chopping motion with hands forward and then a hand stop signal with both hands.**

They took all the ingredients and put them in a big pot. **Draw legs towards the body and press the soles of the feet together to form a pot shape.**

They stirred with their head – **head stirring action.**

They stirred with their shoulders – **shoulder stirring action.**

They stirred with their body – **body stirring action.**

And when the soup was ready they scooped it into a bowl.

One bowl - **Stretch and scoop to one side.**

Two bowls - **Stretch and scoop to the other side.**

And they blew on the soup (blow x 3) until it was just right and then they slurped it down.

Three big slurps.

After that they were so tired they went walk, walk, walk, walk. Skippity-hop, skippity-hop, jump, jump, jump, jump. Stop! (x3) All the way to their beds. And when they reached their beds, they jumped into bed and it wasn't long before you could hear them snoring.

AUTUMN LEAVES

In Aotearoa and Australia most of our indigenous trees are evergreen, in that they will keep their leaves all year round. However, our landscape also contains many exotic trees from the northern hemisphere that are deciduous, losing their leaves in autumn and winter. Our native plants are also changing. Many of them will have produced and opened their seed heads.

These changes are an easy place to begin conversations about seasonal change. If you have a large deciduous tree nearby – make a journey with the tamariki to collect autumn leaves. Spend some time watching the leaves fall (more likely to happen on a day with a bit of wind) and observe how they move on their descent to the earth.

LEAF PILE RACE

If you have access to a deciduous tree, take a couple of hula-hoops or ropes and lay them on the ground (the ropes to form a circle). Form a couple of teams and set a timer. Teams have to heap as many leaves in the hoop in the set time.

THE LEAF AND THE WIND DANCE

This movement exploration can take place outside near the tree or later after collecting leaves, inside.

Ask the children if they have ever seen the wind blow the leaves? Ask if they would like to be like the wind and do a leaf-wind dance with their leaves. They are going to be like the wind.

Each child chooses a leaf. Ask them to find a 'perfect' space to put the leaf on the floor/earth, so that they will have plenty of room for moving. Using music or a percussive instrument/ beat, encourage children to explore the relationship they can have with the leaf, dancing away from, towards, over, under, on top of, around, behind, in front of the leaf etc.

"I wonder who can find a way to dance around their leaf? What about making a shape underneath their leaf? Who can jump around their leaf and I wonder who can travel away from their leaf very quickly and then creep back very slowly/quietly/down low?"

Then ask the children to pick up their leaves and dance them (like the wind) to a new area and place them on the ground/floor again (vary the locomotive movement – skip to a new place, twirl, jump, hop, travel backwards etc). Then repeat again the movement exploration with the leaf stationary.

DANCING THE STORY OF THE AUTUMN LEAVES IN THE GARDEN

This movement story can be used as an extension of the above exploration or as a 'stand-alone' activity. Gather the children together into a group in the centre of the room. If you have any dry leaves encourage the children to drop them and watch them fall. Find words and movement to describe how they fall. If it is autumn, discuss with them what they have seen happening with some of the trees. If not, you can frame the dance as a told story, about a gardener who was working in his garden in autumn.

Once upon a time there was a beautiful garden. (Encourage the children to describe what they think might have been in the garden). The garden was looked after by a gardener. He loved to take care of all the plants, flowers and trees. In the centre of the garden was a huge tree. In summer it was green but in the autumn the leaves turned red, orange, gold and brown and fluttered to the ground. The gardener was very tidy. He liked to rake the leaves up and put them into his compost where they would break down and make delicious food for the plants and trees. But there was something else that loved the leaves: it was the wind. The wind loved to blow the leaves and make them dance - swirling, twirling, leaping and flying. Do you think the gardener liked that? Would you like to dance the story of the gardener, the wind and the leaves?

Explain to the children that the dance will start with all the leaves sitting tightly together in the middle of the room on the tree. When you call out their name, one by one they will fall from the tree and find a place to rest away from the tree. They could even make a 'fallen leaf' shape – flat, curled, pointy etc.

MOVEMENT STORY

Recording available

In the centre of a garden stood a great spreading tree. **Children sit/stand closely next to each other in the centre of the room.**

It was autumn and leaves on the tree had turned red, orange and yellow.

One by one they fell from the branches, down, down, down; down to the ground below and there they made shapes on the ground. **As each child is tapped or their name is said, they leave the group and dance through space and find a new place away from the group and make a shape.**

Along came the gardener and began to rake the leaves together. He raked and rolled them towards each other until they formed a great leafy pile. **Adult comes around and gently taps/rolls each child to that they roll back towards the centre of the room to form a group again.**

When all of a sudden along came the wind and blew the leaves far away from each other, scattering them once again all over the garden. **Group scatters, individuals travel through space, find a new place and make a shape. The sequence of raking up the leaves and the wind blowing is repeated 3 times.**

Finally the gardener came and picked each leaf up and put it in his wheelbarrow and wheeled the leaves to the compost heap. **Adult comes and collects children one at a time into a long 'follow the leader' line. Children copy the leader's movements. The group travels back to the centre and forms a tightly packed group.**

There the leaves wriggled and squirmed and melted back down into the ground, ready to feed the garden next spring. **Group slowly lowers themselves to the ground, wriggling and writhing.**

Notes: With younger children, mats (or leaves) can be spread out around the room before the dance begins, so that the children have a 'place' to dance to. Initially the adult will model the role of the gardener. Later older children might want to take this role themselves and lead the group.

STORIES OF HARVEST

Autumn is the time for harvest. I think there are three important principles of harvest – whatever your harvest might be (it doesn't have to be food).

1. Enjoy and make good use of what you harvest.

2. Share your bounty with others

3. Gratitude – give thanks for what you've got.

KŪMARA – THE FIRST HARVEST

The first cultivated crop in Aotearoa was kūmara bought to these shores by tangata Māori . If you have a garden, I strongly recommend growing kūmara. If you're not sure how – reach out to the kūmara growers in your community. The process is fascinating, the plant is beautiful, and you are paying homage to one of the first cultivated foods of Aotearoa (in Australia you might consider growing yams or something regionally equivalent). Kūmara is planted in spring and harvested in autumn. Harvesting kūmara is finding treasure buried in the earth.

TRADING CIRCLE ADD – ON GAME

Sit in a circle shape. Introduce the idea of trading – exchanging something for something else without using money. I suggest using an object to represent the trade – something plain e.g. a small wooden block that can be passed as each trade is made to signify as a 'turn taker'.

First person:
(I suggest this is initially you)
I grew some apples and I took them to a crop swap and traded them for… pass the block to the next person

Second person:
Some (pears).

Whole group repeats:
Apple for pears, pears for…

Third person:
Some (pumpkins).

Whole group repeats:
Apples for pears, pears for pumpkins, pumpkins for…

Fourth person:
Some plum jam.

Whole group repeats:
Apples for pears, pears for pumpkins, pumpkins for plum jam, plum jam for…

The game continues around the circle with each person adding a new trade and the whole group repeating the sequence of trades. Giving each trade item an action will help with remembering. This is a good game for listening, recall and imagining.

APPLE DUMPLINGS — AN ADAPTED TRADITIONAL ENGLISH FOLKTALE

Recording available ♪

This story is an extension of the trading circle above. I live in a community where we regularly trade food and I also participate in biweekly 'crop swaps'. We live in such a monetized world that it's refreshing to introduce the idea of exchange. You might even want to have a class/centre 'crop swap' as part of your autumn celebrations. Check out the crop swap community at cropswap.co.nz. I learned this story to share at the annual Wakefield Apple Fair in the Nelson area, Te Wai Pounamu/ South Island.

Once upon a time there was an old woman who wanted apple dumplings for her supper. She had plenty of flour and plenty of oil, plenty of sugar, and plenty of spice, but there was one thing she did not have – apples!

But she had plums, a tree full of them, the roundest and reddest that you can imagine; but though you can make marmalade from oranges, kimchi from cabbages, pickles from cucumbers and chutney from marrow – you can't make apples out of plums – and there's no use trying!

The more the old woman thought of the dumplings, the more she wanted some, so she dressed herself in her finest clothes and off she set to find herself some apples. Before she left home, she filled her basket with juicy plums from her plum-tree and said to herself: "There may be those in the world who have apples, and need plums." And as she walked

You can make
Marmalade from oranges
Kimchi from cabbages
Pickles from cucumbers and
Chutney from marrow
But you're plum out of luck
Cause a chicken is no duck
And you can't make apples out of plums

She had not gone very far when she came to a field filled with fine hens and geese. "Ca-ca, quawk, quawk!" There in the midst of them stood a young woman who was feeding them with yellow corn. She nodded pleasantly to the old woman, and the old woman nodded to her, and soon the two were talking as if they had known each other always.

The young woman told the old woman about her birds and the old woman told the young woman about the apple dumplings and the basket of plums which she hoped to exchange for apples.

"You know," said the young woman when she heard this, "there is nothing my children like better than plum jam, but all I can offer is a bag of feathers."

"Well better one pleased, than two disappointed," said the old woman, "and feathers are lighter than plums!"

And so a trade was made. She emptied the plums into the young woman's apron and putting the bag of feathers into her basket walked on as merrily as before singing:

You can make
Marmalade from oranges
Kimchi from cabbages
Pickles from cucumbers and
Chutney from marrow

But you're plum out of luck
Cause a chicken is no duck
And you can't make apples out of plums

By and by the old woman came to a garden of sweet flowers - dahlias, lilies, roses and zinnias -oh, never was there a lovelier garden. The old woman stopped at the gate to admire the flowers, and as she looked she heard a man and a woman arguing.

"Cotton," said the woman.

"Straw," said the man.

"Cotton."

"Straw!"

Back and forth they went until they spied the old woman at the gate.

"Here is one who will settle the matter," said the woman and she called to the old woman: "Good mother, If you were making a cushion for your grandfather's chair would you not stuff it with cotton?"

"No," said the old woman.

"I told you so," cried the man. "Straw is the thing, and there's plenty in the barn."

But the old woman shook her head," I would not stuff the cushion with straw, either," said she, "A feather cushion would be fit for a king, and look," she held up her basket, "I have a basket full of feathers that I'll happily trade you for apples or a bouquet of flowers from your garden."

The man and the woman had no apples, but they were glad to exchange a bouquet from their garden. Oh, never was there a sweeter bouquet.

"A good bargain, and not all of it in the basket," said the old woman, for she was pleased to have stopped the quarrel, and when she had wished the two good fortune and a long life, she went upon her way singing:

You can make
Marmalade from oranges
Kimchi from cabbages
Pickles from cucumbers and
Chutney from marrow
But you're plum out of luck
Cause a chicken is no duck
And you can't make apples out of plums

Now her way was the king's highway, and as she walked along the byway, she met a young lord who was dressed in his finest clothes, for he was going to see his love. He would have been the handsomest young man as ever the sun shone on had it not been for a terrible frown that furrowed his face.

"A fair day and a good road," said the old woman, as he passed by.

"Fair or foul, good or bad, 'tis all the same to me," said he, "when the court jeweller has forgotten to send the ring he promised, and I must go to my love with empty hands."

"You shall have a gift for your love," said the old woman, "though I may never have apple dumplings." And she took the bouquet from her basket and gave it to the man which pleased him so much that the frown disappeared, and a smile spread across his face, and now he was the handsomest young man as ever the sun shone upon.

"Fair trade is no robbery," said he, and he unfastened a golden chain from round his neck and gave it to the old woman, and went on his way holding his bouquet with great care.

The old woman was delighted. "Well with this golden chain I might buy all the apples in the king's market, and then have something to spare," she said to herself, as she hurried away toward town as fast as her feet could carry her singing:

You can make
Marmalade from oranges
Kimchi from cabbages
Pickles from cucumbers and

Chutney from marrow
But you're plum out of luck
Cause a chicken ain't no duck
And you can't make apples out of plums

But as she entered the town the first people she came upon were a mother and her children, standing in a doorway, their faces were as sorrowful as her own was happy.

"What is the matter?" she asked as soon as she reached them.

"You're kind enough to ask, old woman. We've eaten our last crust of bread and don't have a penny in the house to buy more."

"Well, never shall it be said of me that I ate apple dumplings for supper while my neighbours lacked bread," and she put the golden chain into the mother's hand and hurried on without waiting for thanks.

"Wait, old woman," called the mother. "We've little to give you, for what you have done for us, but please take this little dog, whose company will keep loneliness from your house, and our thanks goes with it."

The old woman did not have the heart to say 'no' to the puppy, so into the basket went the little dog, and very snugly he lay there.

"A bag of feathers for a basket of plums; a bouquet of flowers for a bag of feathers; a golden chain for a bouquet of flowers; and a puppy for a golden chain; all the world is give and take,

and who knows but that I may have my apple dumpling yet," said the old woman as she turned and left the town.

And sure enough she had not gone a quarter of a mile from the town when, right before her, she saw an apple tree as full of apples as her plum tree was full of plums. It grew in front of a house as much like her own and on the porch of the house sat a little old man.

"A fine tree of apples," called the old woman as soon as she was within speaking distance of him.

"Aye, but apple trees and apples are poor company when a man is growing old," said the old man, "and I would give them all if I had even so much as a little dog to bark on my door-step."

"Woof, woof," called the dog in the old woman's basket, and in less time than it takes to tell this story he was sitting at the feet of the old man and the old woman was on her way home with a basket of apples.

"If you try long enough and hard enough, you can always have apple dumplings for supper," said the old woman making a double batch – one for her and one for the old man. And she ate those dumplings for her supper and every very last crumb was yum!

RECIPE

You might like to have a go at making your own apple dumplings. I can assure you, they are yum!

INGREDIENTS

DOUGH

2 cups of flour
4 tablespoons of coconut oil (or similar)
2 ½ teaspoons of baking powder
1 teaspoon salt
Up to 1 cup of water

FILLING

2- 3 apples
1 cup of brown sugar
½ cup water
4 tablespoons coconut oil (or similar)
1 tsp of vanilla
1 tsp of cinnamon

INSTRUCTIONS

1. Combine dry ingredients of the dough and then rub in oil/veg butter with your fingers, then slowly add water until you make a firm dough

2. Divide into 10 parts, roll each part into a round circle
3. Chop and cook apples a little – don't make them mushy
4. Combine all the other filling ingredients and heat
5. Tip these over the apples and leave them to marinate
6. Spoon apple mixture onto dough circles and pinch them into little apple pouches. Place into a baking dish and tip the rest of the liquid over the top
7. Bake in a moderate oven for 15 – 30 minutes. Share and repeat. Enjoy!

HALLOWEEN – SAMHAIN
(SUMMER'S END)

Autumn is the time for northern seasonal celebrations such as Halloween. If you want to carve a pumpkin or a hue (the original cucurbit bought by early Polynesian voyagers to Aoteroa), now is the time to do it.

The following is a great sing along story that can be extended into pumpkin carving and making pumpkin soup. I often ask the children about the sorts of plants the granddaughter might have growing in her garden and what kind of food could be made from those plants. For those of you who are musically adventurous you can actually sing the two 'old woman' songs simultaneously at the end of the story. 'Through the forest I go, go, go' and 'Roll my pumpkin' - a fun musical activity for older children.

ROLL MY PUMPKIN
AN ADAPTED TRADITIONAL IRANIAN FOLKTALE

Recording available ♪

I learnt this story for the annual Harvest Fayre – held by our local Steiner Kindergarten.

Once there was a dark, deep forest. On one side of the forest lived a girl with a garden full of good things to eat. On the other side lived her grandmother, a little old woman with her big, white dog.

One day the little old woman said to her dog, "Big White Dog, today I'm going to visit my granddaughter, she's invited me for lunch. But I can't take you because you'll dig up the garden. So here's a bone. Now stay home and be good." And with that the old woman set off through the forest singing:

> **Through the forest I go, go, go**
> **Sometimes fast and sometimes slow**
> **Through the forest I go, go, go**
> **To see my lovely granddaughter**

Now who should she meet but a hungry fox.

"Where are you going?" asked the fox, licking his lips.

"I'm on my way to visit my granddaughter," the old woman replied.

"Oh no you're not," said the fox, "because I'm going to eat you up."

"Oh no!" said the old woman, "That would not be a good idea because now I am thin and boney. Wait until I return from my granddaughter's house where she will feed me lots of fine food, then I'll be fat and juicy."

"Very well, said the fox, "but make sure you come back this way."

"I promise," said the old woman and continued on her way singing:

Through
the forest I go, go, go
Sometimes fast and sometimes slow
Through the forest I go, go, go
To see my lovely granddaughter

Now who should she meet but a hungry wolf with sharp teeth.

"Where are you going?" asked the wolf with his sharp, sharp teeth.

"I'm on my way to visit my granddaughter", the old woman replied.

"Oh no you're not," said the wolf, "because I'm going to eat you up."

"Oh no!" said the old woman, "That would not be a good idea because now I am thin and boney. Wait until I return from my granddaughter's house where she will feed me lots of fine food, then I'll be fat and juicy."

"Very well, said the wolf, "but make sure you come back this way."

"I promise," said the old woman and continued on her way singing:

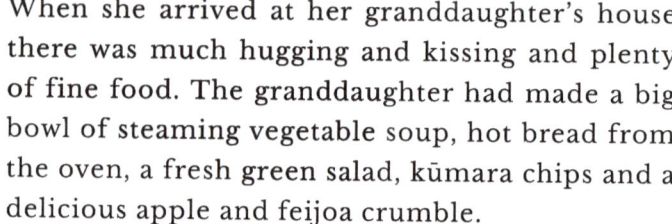

Through the forest I go, go, go
Sometimes fast and sometimes slow
Through the forest I go, go, go
To see my lovely granddaughter

Now at the centre of the woods, in a cave, lived a monster. He had a big snotty nose, huge hairy ears and sharp, sharp claws. And when he heard the singing he came out of his cave and stood on the path and shouted, "Where are you going?"

The old woman replied, "I'm off to see my granddaughter."

"Oh no you're not," said the monster, "because I'm going to eat you up.

"Oh no!" said the old woman, "That would not be a good idea because now I am thin and boney. Wait until I return from my granddaughter's house where she will feed me lots of fine food, then I'll be fat and juicy."

"Very well," said the monster, "but make sure you come back or else I'll find you and eat you up."

"I promise," said the old woman and continued on her way.

Through the forest I go, go, go
Sometimes fast and sometimes slow
Through the forest I go, go, go
To see my lovely granddaughter

When she arrived at her granddaughter's house there was much hugging and kissing and plenty of fine food. The granddaughter had made a big bowl of steaming vegetable soup, hot bread from the oven, a fresh green salad, kūmara chips and a delicious apple and feijoa crumble.

The old woman gobbled it all up and the two of them sat and talked and ate, and talked and ate and talked and ate. Until the old woman said, "My, my – how time flies. I'd be best getting home. My dog will be missing me."

Then she stopped. "There is one problem though. There's a fox who's promised to eat me."

"Oh no!" said the granddaughter

"Well two problems actually – there's a wolf who's promised to eat me."

"What trouble!" said the granddaughter.

"Well three problems really – there's a monster who's promised to eat me and if I don't go back, he said he'll find me and gobble me up."

"Well this won't do," said her granddaughter, "I have an idea."

And into her garden she went and picked the most enormous pumpkin. She cut off the top and scooped out all the seeds and flesh until the pumpkin was hollow.

"Now, in you go grandmother!"

And the old woman hopped into the pumpkin and her granddaughter fastened the lid on top.

"Now don't get out until you're safely home." said the granddaughter and with that she gave the pumpkin a push and off the pumpkin rolled. Inside the pumpkin the old woman sang:

>Roll my pumpkin, roll my pumpkin
>Rolling all day long
>Roll my pumpkin, roll my pumpkin
>As we sing this song
>Roll my pumpkin, roll my pumpkin
>Rolling all day long
>Roll my pumpkin, roll my pumpkin
>As we sing this song

The pumpkin rolled out the gate, along the path and into the forest. It hadn't rolled far, when who should she meet but the hungry fox.

"Have you seen a little old lady?" asked the fox

"No, I'm just a singing, rolling pumpkin," replied the old woman and rolled on past the fox singing:

>Roll my pumpkin, roll my pumpkin
>Rolling all day long
>Roll my pumpkin, roll my pumpkin
>As we sing this song
>Roll my pumpkin, roll my pumpkin
>Rolling all day long
>Roll my pumpkin, roll my pumpkin
>As we sing this song

A little further into the forest, when who should she meet, but the wolf with the sharp, sharp teeth.

"Have you seen a little old lady?" asked the wolf.

"No, I'm just a singing, rolling pumpkin," replied the old woman and rolled on past the wolf singing:

>Roll my pumpkin, roll my pumpkin
>Rolling all day long
>Roll my pumpkin, roll my pumpkin
>As we sing this song
>Roll my pumpkin, roll my pumpkin
>Rolling all day long
>Roll my pumpkin, roll my pumpkin
>As we sing this song

At last the pumpkin rolled past the cave of the monster and out the monster came and said,

"Have you seen a little old lady?"

"No, I'm just a singing, rolling pumpkin." replied the old woman.

"A singing pumpkin!" said the monster, "This singing pumpkin sounds a lot like the old woman who passed through the forest."

"I don't know any old woman," said the pumpkin, "I'm just a rolling pumpkin."

"I think you are the little old woman who is trying to trick me." growled the monster, "Now come out of the pumpkin or I'll smash the pumpkin."

"All right!" replied the old woman, "But it's a magic pumpkin and I can only come out if you say the magic word."

"Please, come out," said the monster.

"No, not that magic word!"

"Thank you, come out," said the monster.

"No not that magic word, you have to say – Coooooome heeeeeeere myyyyyyy biiiiiiiig whiiiiiite dooooooog."

"That's a very strange magic word," said the monster.

"Well it's the only one that works," replied the old woman.

"Alright!" said the monster, "Coooooome heeeeeeere myyyyyyy biiiiiiiig whiiiiiite dooooooog."

"I'm very old and deaf and can't hear you, can you say it louder?"

"Coooooome heeeeeeere myyyyyyy biiiiiiiig whiiiiiite dooooooog."

"Louder and faster!"

"Coooooome heeeeeeere myyyyyyy biiiiiiiig whiiiiiite dooooooog."

"You're going to have to shout it three times very fast."

"Come here my big, white dog! Come here my big, white dog! Come here my big, white dog!"

When all of a sudden there was the sound of barking and along the path came the old woman's big white dog, who was also very hungry and chased the monster all way down the hill and far, far away. And the old woman in the pumpkin rolled all the way home singing:

Roll my pumpkin, roll my pumpkin
Rolling all day long
Roll my pumpkin, roll my pumpkin
As we sing this song
Roll my pumpkin, roll my pumpkin
Rolling all day long
Roll my pumpkin, roll my pumpkin
As we sing this song

And when she got home the old woman made a hearty pumpkin soup which just goes to show that not only are vegetables healthy and yummy they might just save your life.

THANK YOU SONG

EXPRESSING GRATITUDE

Recording available

Giving thanks is part of any harvest celebration. Here is a simple gratitude song that can be shared. Group sits in a circle and passes a heart shape or another turn-signifying-object around the circle. When the song stops the person with the 'turn-taker' says something they are grateful for. Alternatively turns can be taken randomly without a turn taker.

Thank you, thank you for the earth and the sea
Thank you, thank you for the birds and the trees
We are so lucky for all that we share
Thank you thank you, please know that I care

A BATTY HALLOWEEN/ SAMHAIN

Bats are animals commonly associated with Halloween and just so happen to be native mammals of both Australia, Aotearoa/New Zealand and many of the Pacific Islands. In Aotearoa they are our only land mammals and are certainly worthy of celebrating. Bats prove to be quite popular with young children because of the superhero characters Batman and Batwoman. But bats in themselves are ecological super heroes – devouring tonnes of insects on a nightly basis, providing guano and pollinating all manner of plants.

SIMPLE CIRCLE GAME/SONG
Recording available ♪

Rat-a-tat- bat
What is that?
Flying high
Flying low
Rat-a-tat- bat
Night is done
Find your roost
And choose someone

This is a simple circle game played with a bat puppet or with a child taking the role of the bat. The group sits in a circle on the floor. The person who is the bat flies on the outside of the circle while the rest of the group sing the chant. When the chant ends the bat lands (if a puppet) on someone's shoulder or taps someone on the shoulder and they take the turn of being the bat.

WHY BATS HANG UPSIDE DOWN

AN ADAPTED TRADITIONAL STORY FROM SUDAN

Recording available

I learnt this story to share at a Bat-a-thon when our New Zealand bat, pekapeka-tou-roa was running for manu/bird of the year. This story can be introduced by asking children what they might already know about bats. They might talk about them hanging upside down, being awake at night, having wings, what they like to eat (Australasian bats eat fruit and insects – not blood!). Use these ideas to inform the story and also demonstrate that things change.

For you see, bats didn't always hang upside down and they haven't always been nocturnal. Once upon a time bats were day creatures, living upright with the birds and bees up in the tree. But then one day there was a party...

Party, party did you hear about the party
Party, party did you hear about the party
A party over here — a party over there
A party on (Waiheke/or other place) —
                                   a party everywhere

Yep, there was going to be a party and everyone was invited - everyone that was a mammal.

Are you a mammal? Were you born alive? Did you drink your mother's milk? Is your blood warm? OK – you're a mammal – so you were invited to the party and bat was a mammal, so on the day of the party bat readied herself.

She licked her fur until it shone, she flossed and polished her teeth, she painted her toenails and then she headed off to the...

Party, party did you hear about the party
Party, party did you hear about the party
A party over here — a party over there
A party on (Waiheke/ or other place) —
                                   a party everywhere

And when she arrived there was a dog (or another familiar mammal) welcoming all the mammals to the party.

"What's a bat like you doing in a place like this?"

"I'm here for the party. I'm so excited."

"The mammal party?"

"Yep – the mammal party – that's me – Ms Mammal."

"Hang on – what are those under your arms?"

"What?"

"Those wingy things?"

"These - these are just my flabby bits."

"They look like wings to me and I don't know of any mammals who fly, so you're not a mammal, this party's not for you."

"But…"

"No buts, no bats!"

Poor bat. She turned and flew back to her roost high among the trees and she stood there on the branch and wept and her tears rolled down her fur until her perch became wet and slippery and – whoops – she fell upside down and her tears fell to the earth like rain.

Well when the birds heard of the success of the mammal party, they decided to have one of their own. The word went out that there was going to be a party…

Party, party did you hear about the party
Party, party did you hear about the party
A party of here — a party over there
A party on Waiheke — a party everywhere

Bat perked up when she heard about the bird party – perhaps she'd be more welcome there. On the appointed day, bat readied herself. She washed and blow dried her wings and headed off to the party. And there was a Hawk (or another familiar bird) greeting the guests.

"Hi there Hawk."

"Hello Bat. How can I help you?"

"I've come for the party."

"The bird party?"

"Yeah look at my wings, I'm a bird, a strange bird but a bird nonetheless."

"You have fur and teeth?"

"It's fake fur (no teeth bat)."

"I'm sorry Bat – you're not a bird – this party isn't for you."

Sadly the bat turned away and flew, not back to her roost but to the dark heart of an old tree where neither the mammals nor the birds would find her. She wept and wept, until her perch grew slippery and her tears fell to the ground like rain until whoops - she spun upside.

But then she stopped crying and she thought – "Hey when you're upside down you see the world differently and that's special. I might have wings, fur and teeth but that doesn't make me wrong, it makes me unique. I'm going to celebrate myself - just the way I am."

And from that time on every night bat flies out with her bat – friends for a bat party, using her super echolocation powers to navigate in the dark and every morning she flies home to roost upside down – which for her, is the right way up.

Note: This story is a great way of opening a conversation about inclusion and how we respond to difference.

UPSIDE–DOWN DANCE

Recording available

You will need space markers, music with a repeating ABAB pattern or two different sounding instruments (e.g. drum and triangle) that can indicate day and night. A space marker can be a thin foam mat, carpet square, a shoe or something safe to have on the floor while people are moving about, that marks a place for the child. Children begin on or close to their space marker. The space marker is used to distinguish between self-space and general space. In self-space we explore an idea non-locomotivity, and in general space we explore the idea locomotivity. Find a place in the room for your mat.

Once upon a time in the ngahere, in a big old tree/cave, there lived a bat. During the daytime this bat stayed in her roost and at night she came out to hunt. While she was resting she hung upside down. Can you find an upside down way to be on your mat?

Children travel around the room to one sound/instrument and return to their space marker when they hear the other sound/instrument or when the music changes.

When travelling around the room encourage the children to move at different levels (high, mid, low), speeds (fast and slow), directions (forwards, backwards, sideways), using different sized wings (big flapping, small flapping), etc.

When they return to their space markers, challenge them to find different ways to be upside down: Can you try hanging the top part of your body from your hips up, upside down? Can you lie upside down? Can you balance upside down? Alternate being upside down on the space marker (day-time) with travelling/flying away from the space marker and around the room (night-time).

Finding something with our ears

Some people say 'blind as a bat' when they want to say that someone cannot find something or can't see very well, but bats can see as well as you and I can in the daytime. Like humans they can't see very well with their eyes in the dark, which is a problem because they are nocturnal and hunt at night. Their special way of 'seeing' at night is by hearing with sound, which is called echolocation. When animals echolocate they send out a sound, which bounces off other objects creating sound waves. Those sound waves help them navigate in the dark.

Listening game

You will need an instrument/object that makes a sustained sound – a bell, sound bowl, triangle, chimes, etc. Ask the children to close their eyes, then move away from the group and play the instrument/object. Ask the children if they can point in the direction of the sound.

Echolocation game

Sit as a group in a circle in the centre of the room. Practise making clicking sounds with your tongue or finger snaps/claps (not everyone can tongue click).

One person (A) becomes the bat and wears a blindfold. Another person (B) becomes the bat's kai/food and quietly goes somewhere else in the room.

When the person who is bat (A) clicks, (B) clicks back like an echo. (A) clicks again and (B) responds. (A) listens and clicks and moves towards where they think (B) is. The clicking and responding continues until (A) finds (B). It's a good idea to have a 'guide' accompany (A) to make sure they remain safe and don't fall or lose their balance. They can walk alongside (A) without interfering and only touch (A) if they are unsafe.

BAT ACTION SONG

Recording available ♪

Once upon a time in the ngahere, in a big,
old tree/rākau there lived a bat — pekapeka

This bat was not so nui/big
In fact she was iti bitty
With a short little whiore/tail
And ngā pakihau/wings that flap

She had a special talent
She could hunt in the dark
She could echolocate with her taringa/ears
and her waha/mouth

She went flying, she went flying
Flying through the night
She was flitting, she was flapping
Hoping to catch a bite

And when a moth flew by
She said, "yum, yum!
Soon that moth's going to be in my tum."
She was clicking and listening
With her sonar radar

She was clicking & listening
Catching the insects on her path/ara

OOum!

She went flying, she went flying
Flying through the night
She was flitting, she was flapping
Hoping to catch a bite

And when a beetle flew by
She said, "yum, yum!
Soon that beetle's going to be in my tum."

She was clicking and listening
With her sonar radar
She was clicking & listening
Catching the insects on her path/ara

OOum!

She went flying, she went flying
Flying through the night
She was flitting, she was flapping
Hoping to catch a bite

And when a mozzie flew by
She said, "yum, yum!

Soon that mozzie's going to be in my tum"

She was clicking and listening
With her sonar radar
She was clicking & listening
Catching the insects on her path/ara

OOum!

And now her tummy's full and the moon has
gone to bed
Back to her roost she flies
To rest her sleepy head

Her friends are waiting there
Hanging from their feet
With their wings wrapped away
They close their eyes and sleep

She is sleeping (e moi), upside down sleeping
(e moi)
While the sun is shining bright
She is resting, she is waiting
To hunt again in the night

Pōmārie pekapeka

Please see appendix for additional links to bat resources.

WINTER – HŌTOKE

Ka rere ngā purapura a Matariki.

Māori Whakataukī

The seeds of Matariki are falling,

referring to the first snow.

Māori Proverb

The fires burn and the kettles sing,

and earth sinks to rest until next spring.

Clyde Watson

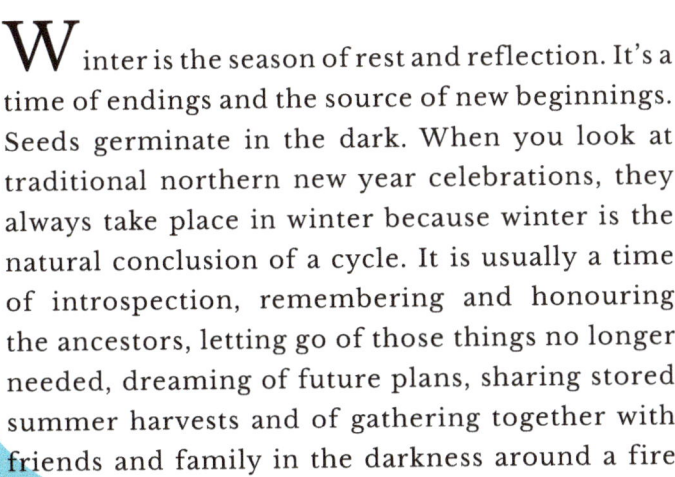

Winter is the season of rest and reflection. It's a time of endings and the source of new beginnings. Seeds germinate in the dark. When you look at traditional northern new year celebrations, they always take place in winter because winter is the natural conclusion of a cycle. It is usually a time of introspection, remembering and honouring the ancestors, letting go of those things no longer needed, dreaming of future plans, sharing stored summer harvests and of gathering together with friends and family in the darkness around a fire to sing and tell stories. The reduction of light can induce depressive states and celebrations form an important role in creating resilience and maintaining well-being.

Like many others, I have welcomed and been hugely excited about the renaissance of the Māori New Year, Matariki/Pūanga. It is a celebration unique to Aotearoa, honouring mātauranga Māori, but it also is a celebration that literally makes 'sense'. The celebration is confirmed in our experience of the season.

LAYING THE TABLE FOR WINTER

I wonder what the qualities of winter are?

Suggestions: Rest, death, reflection, endings, return of light

I wonder which plants we usually see/use in winter?

Suggestions: Kawakawa, kumarāhou, calendulas, camellias

I wonder which foods we have available to eat in winter?

Suggestions: Hot soups, preserved food, citrus, honey, leafy greens, broccoli, cabbage, cauliflower

I wonder which animals we see in winter?

Suggestions: Lamprey/korokoro, new lambs and calves are born later in winter, young eels arrive back to the shores of Aotearoa and begin making their way back to the bodies of fresh water

I wonder who the atua/deities that can be associated with winter are?

Suggestions: Hine-nui-te-pō, Hecate, Persephone, Hades

WINTER SONG

Recording available ♪

**The wheel keeps turning round and round
The leaves have fallen to the ground
The fires burn long as the days grow short
Persephone returned to Hades court**

Pauline Down 'To Grace the Earth'

A FOOT STORY

THE TWO GECKOS IN A WINTER WONDERLAND

Once upon a time there were two geckos, and when this story started, they were fast asleep, snoring. **Legs stretched out straight in front of the body, toes pointing down to the floor and flexing back towards the chest to the rhythm of the snores.**

And while they were sleeping and snoring, outside the snow was falling. **Stretch arms up above head and lower them, with fingers moving like falling snow.**

When one little gecko woke up and said, "Hooray, what shall we do today?" **Lift your right leg and shake.**

He tried to wake up his friend, "Wake up! Wake up!" **Tap left leg with right leg.**

But his friend was fast asleep, so the little gecko went and fetched an alarm clock. **Left leg continues to point and flex. Right leg bends and tip toes out to the side, level with the hip and returns to front centre. Both legs stretched out straight in front of the body.**

The alarm clock went, "Brrrrrring." But the little gecko still slept. **Shake your whole body gently.**

So the alarm clock rang louder, "Brrrrring." But still the gecko slept. **Shake the whole body a little more vigorously.**

So the alarm clock rang as loud as it could, "Brrrrring." **Shake your whole body with force.**

And the little gecko jumped up, "Hooray!" **Lift your left foot into the air and return to the floor.**

"Hooray!" said her friend. "What shall we do today?" **Turn feet towards each other, and wriggle each foot in turn as it speaks.**

"Let's go and see the snow. But first, let's do our exercises." So the two little geckos went point and flex and point and flex. **Point and flex feet.**

Round and around and around and around and then the other way. **Ankle rotations (turn feet in small circles from the ankle) of both feet in both directions.**

Then in and out and in and out and in and out. **In a sitting position jump feet apart and then back together again three times.**

"Before we go outside we'll need to dress warmly." So one little gecko put on a woolly hat on their head, warm gloves on their hands, waterproof boots on their feet and a snuggly scarf around their neck. **As each item of clothing is mentioned, act out putting them on the various** body parts.

The other little gecko put on a woolly hat on their head, warm gloves on their hands, waterproof boots on their feet and a snuggly scarf around their neck. **As each item of clothing is mentioned, act out putting them on the various body parts.**

And then off they set outside. They went walk, walk, walk, walk. Skippity-hop, skippity-hop, jump, jump, jump, jump. Stop! (x3) **Rhythm of different steps performed using the feet in a sitting position, with bent knees.**

And they came to where the snow began. It was white and bright and cold. They reached down with one hand and scooped up a hand fall of snow, rolled it into a snowball and threw it. **Start with one arm. Reach to the same side as the arm to the floor, just below your hip as if picking up a handful of snow. Roll it in front of you with both hands and then 'throw' stretching your arm towards the opposite foot.**

They reached down with the other hand and scooped up a hand fall of snow, rolled it into a snowball and threw it. **Start with the other arm. Reach to the same side as the arm to the floor, just below your hip as if picking up a handful of snow. Roll it in front of you with both hands and then 'throw' stretching your arm towards the opposite foot.**

They reached down with both hands and scooped up two hand falls of snow, rolled it into a bigger snowball and threw it. **Start with both arms simultaneously to your sides as if picking up a handfuls of snow. Roll it in front of you with both hands and then 'throw' stretching both arms towards your feet.**

The two little geckos decided to walk through the snow and up a hill. The snow was crunchy and deep and tricky to walk in. They went crunch, crunch, crunch, crunch. Slippity-hop, slippity-hop, jump, jump, jump, jump. Stop! (x3) **Rhythm of different steps performed using the feet in a sitting position, with bent knees.**

At the top of the hill they stopped and looked back down the slippery white slope. They turned and slid all the way back down the slope. Weeeeeee! **In a seated position with bent knees, lift the legs off the floor, engaging stomach muscles and lift arms above the head and call out, "weeeeeeee!"**

When they reached the bottom they climbed up the hill again. **They went crunch, crunch, crunch, crunch. Slippity-hop, slippity-hop, jump, jump, jump, jump. Stop! (x3). Rhythm of different steps performed using the feet in a sitting position, with bent knees.**

At the top of the hill they stopped and slipped back down the slippery white slope. Weeeeeee! **In a seated position with bent knees, lift the legs off the floor, engaging stomach muscles and lift arms above the head and call out, "weeeeeeee!"**

It was so much fun that they did it one more time. Up the hill they went crunch, crunch,

crunch, crunch. Slippity-hop, slippity-hop, jump, jump, jump, jump. Stop! (x3) **Rhythm of different steps performed using the feet in a sitting position, with bent knees.**

And back down the hill on their bottoms. **In a seated position with bent knees, lift the legs off the floor, engaging stomach muscles and lift arms above the head and call out, "weeeeeeee!"**
They were too tired to climb back up the hill and so they decided they would build a snow person. They scooped up a big armful of snow and rolled it round and round and round to make a big ball for the snow person's bottom. **Scoop both arms to the sides of the body and hold them in a round shape in front of the body. Then circle the body from the hips in a seated position, moving the body forward and around in a large circle.**
Then they scooped a middle sized armful of snow and rolled it round and round and round to make a middle sized ball for the snow person's middle. **Scoop both arms to the sides of the body and hold them in a round shape in front of the body. This time roll the shoulders in a circular motion   first in one direction and then the other.**
Then they scooped a small sized armful of snow and rolled it round and round and round to make a small sized ball for the snow person's head. **Scoop both arms to the sides of the body and hold them in a round shape in front of the body. This time roll the head in a gentle circular motion   first in one direction and then the other.**
Then they stacked the three balls on top of each

other – the largest at the bottom, then the middle sized one and on the top the smallest. **Touch the thighs, the torso and head to indicate the three snowballs.**

Then they made two eyes from rocks, a nose from a pinecone, a smiling mouth from a leaf and used two sticks for arms. **Touch the parts of the body as they are described, stretching arms to the side for the two sticks.** (x 3)

Now their snowperson was finished but it was a sunny winter day and as the sun shone down on the snow person, they began to melt until all that was left was a watery puddle. **Slowly 'melt' the body down towards the floor and lie fully relaxed on your back.**

The two geckos lay on their backs in what was left of the snow and lifted their arms and legs up and down and made snow angels. **Lying on the ground, move arms and legs in and out along the floor.**

Now the geckos were all wet and cold and they hurried back to the house and the warm fire. They went walk, walk, walk, walk. Skippity-hop, skippity-hop, jump, jump, jump, jump. Stop!   (x 3). **Rhythm of different steps performed using the feet in a sitting position, with bent knees.**

When they reached their home they took off their hats, their gloves, their boots and their scarves. They stood by the fire and warmed   their   hands.

rub hands together

They warmed their faces. **rub your cheeks**

They warmed their arms. **rub your arms**

and they warmed their legs. **rub your legs**

Then they took a big puffy marshmallow and stuck it on a stick and heated it over the fire. **Join arms at the front of the body in a circle shape. Lift arms straight up over the head and join hands in a prayer position. Then lower arms towards the feet.**

When the marshmallow was melted they gobbled it down. It was so delicious they took another big puffy marshmallow and stuck it on a stick and heated it over the fire. **Join arms at the front of the body in a circle shape. Lift arms straight up over the head and join hands in a prayer position. Then lower arms towards the feet.**

They thought they would have one last one. They took their last big puffy marshmallow and stuck it on a stick and heated it over the fire. **Join arms at the front of the body in a circle shape. Lift arms straight up over the head and join hands in a prayer position. Then lower arms towards the feet.**

Now their tummies were full, they were tired and they jumped into bed and it wasn't long before they had fallen fast asleep. **Bend knees in a seated position and lift from one side to the other. Stretch legs out straight in front of you and point and flex feet to the rhythm of the snoring.**

THE ELEMENT OF FIRE

In the depth of winter we turn our attention to warmth and being warm. It's a natural time to talk about how we keep warm and the primal connection we have to the old magic of fire. I'm a fan of making fire with children but realise that this might not always be possible given the many health and safety constraints.

However, if making an outdoor fire is an option, be it in a fire-pit or brazier, winter is certainly the safest time to light a fire. Always have a bucket of water/hose ready nearby and be sure to talk to children about fire safety before the fire is lit. Cooking food on the fire and sharing stories/songs around the fire are ancient human practices and deeply nourishing activities to partake in. Why not make a celebration of it and invite the families/whānau of your tamariki for a mid-winter/Matariki celebration.

Another great thing about having a fire is to share stories *about* fire. Every culture has fire stories because its discovery for humans was such a game changer. There are theories that speculate that we were tamed by fire, and our social skills honed so that we had a place with others around the fire. The best-known fire story in Aotearoa is the pūrākau of Māui and Mahuika, which many of you may be familiar with (there is a link to this story on page 128). Māui becomes curious about where fire comes from which results in a visit to his grandmother, the fire goddess Mahuika. In many ways fire is like our curiosity – it can illuminate and warm us but also cause pain and destruction.

I have explored the four elements – earth, air, fire and water – in a storytelling and music programme called Elemental. Some of the material shared here comes from that collection. Here, I use the image of the earth mother/Gaia/Papatūānuku and her necklace as a starting point to introduce the element of fire. If you are interested in the entire programme visit *imagined-worlds.net*

Questions to consider to provoke a conversation about the nature of fire

I wonder what fire is?

I wonder where we find fire?

I wonder who needs fire?

I wonder why we have fire?

CHANT

Recording available ♪

Gaia has necklace on it are four beads
These are the four things that all life needs
Earth: la, la, la, la, la , la
Air: ya, ya, ya, ya, ya, ya
Fire: ra, ra, ra, ra, ra, ra
Water: Va, va, va,va, va, va

FIRE SONG

Recording available ♪

Warmth in my body
Sun in the sky
Volcanoes of the earth
They all are fire

Fire keeps us warm
Fire gives us light
But you've got to be careful
To treat the fire right

Cause it burns — ra,ra,ra,ra!

RAINBOW BIRD

A NORTHERN ABORIGINAL AUSTRALIAN STORY FROM THE DALABON PEOPLE OF THE BESWICK RESERVE

Recording available

This story came to me through UK based storyteller, Eric Maddern, who worked amongst the Dalabon people. Born in New Zealand, I grew up in Australia and the first stories I recall being shared with me were traditional, Australian Aboriginal stories translated into picture book format (Dick Roughsey's picture books and *Djugurba: Tales from the Spirit Time*). These stories were formative in fostering my love of traditional stories.

Long ago in Dreamtime when the world was still new, there lived a rough, tough Crocodile Man with sharp teeth and a long slapping tail. He was big and mean and scary. And he had one thing that no one else had: fire!

Sometimes he held it in his foot, sometimes he breathed it from his mouth, sometimes he flicked it with his tail. He liked to play with the fire. But he didn't like to share. That fire was his and his alone.

Animal people were often cold and they always had to eat their food raw. They would ask Crocodile Man, "Please Crocodile Man, will you share your fire with us?"

But Crocodile Man just snapped and snarled chasing the animal people away, shouting, "I'm boss of fire, I'm boss of fire."

Bird Woman lived in a tree high above Crocodile Man. She was often cold and had to eat her fish and lizards raw. She watched Crocodile Man chasing the other animal people away and felt sorry for them.

"Please Crocodile Man, won't you share just a little bit of your fire?"

"I'm the boss of fire, go away!" snapped Crocodile Man.

"If I had fire I'd share it with you," said Bird Woman.

But all Crocodile Man would say was, "I'm the boss of fire."

Bird Woman didn't give up, she watched and she waited, but Crocodile Man always sat guarding his fire, making sure no one else could have any.

One day as Bird Woman watched Crocodile Man, she saw that his eyes were growing heavy, his great big head was nodding and then he opened his huge mouth filled with sharp teeth and gave a mighty "yawwwwwwwn" and then he fell fast asleep.

At last, Bird Woman saw her chance. Quickly but very quietly she flew down towards the fire. Crocodile Man had his great leathery tail wrapped around it, but Bird Woman was small and fast enough to snatch two fire sticks. Crocodile Man opened his eyes just in time to see Bird Woman fly away. He chased her and snapped but it was too late; Bird Woman had taken his fire.

"I'm boss of fire, I'm boss of fire," he roared.

From the safety of the high branches in the tree, Bird Woman called, "You're not the boss anymore, Crocodile Man. I've got your fire and I'm going to share it."

Then Bird Woman did a little dance and put the fire sticks in her tail and changed into Rainbow Bird. Rainbow Bird Woman flew off, and hid the fire in the hearts of some chosen trees, so that everyone could share fire.

The animal people learned that by rubbing the wood of the trees together they could make fire of their own. They could cook their food, keep warm and light their way at night.

Rainbow Bird flew back to Crocodile Man and said, "Because you wouldn't share your fire, you will have to stay in a place where there is no fire. In the wet swampy water."

And that's where crocodile man still lives today. His fire has gone, but he still growls and snaps and says, " I'm boss, I'm boss."

Rainbow Bird still lives high in the trees. You might see her fire sometimes, in the bright blaze of her beautiful tail feathers.

Please see the appendix for links to additional fire stories from Aotearoa and Australia.

CIRCLE GAME EXTENSION OF THE STORY

One person is chosen as Crocodile Man (who has the fire stick), and one person is Bird Woman. The rest of the group form a big circle around Crocodile Man, who hides his eyes and pretends to be asleep. As the chant is sung by the group, Bird Woman creeps around the outside of the circle and steals the fire stick/s. When she does, the Crocodile Man chases her. They run around the circle and Bird Woman must make it back to her place before he catches her.

Round and round bird woman creeps
Crocodile man is fast asleep
The fire is there for her to take
Unless the Crocodile Man awakes

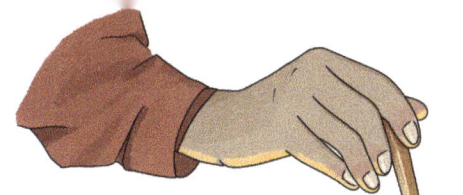

MOVEMENT GAME

Recording available

To begin with, one person is chosen/volunteers to be Bird Woman. She takes the fire stick. The rest of the group form a large circle. While the music is playing, Bird Woman does her fire dance in the centre of the circle. After she does this the other children make tree shapes with their bodies. Bird Woman chooses someone and dances towards them. She gives the fire sticks to them. They then become the Bird Woman dancer in the centre of the circle. Guide the child taking the role of Bird Woman to choose an interesting shaped tree to hide her firesticks in.

SINGING FOR YOUR SUPPER

Recording available

This time of year is traditional for feasting on the saved harvest of summer. You can't feast everyday but you can have hot soup! Making and eating food together is such a unifying activity whether you do it literally or imaginatively.

Ask the children to sit on the floor in a circle. The plate acts as the 'turn taker' i.e. the person holding the plate when the song stops, takes the turn. Like the game 'Pass the parcel' the plate is handed around while the song is sung by the group. The person who has the plate when the song finishes, gets to imagine what kind of food is on the plate. The plate is then placed in the centre of the circle and everyone can take some 'imagined food to share'. Then repeat the process.

Hungry, hungry, I am hungry
What food shall we share today
Hungry, hungry, I am hungry
My favourite food is on this plate

KŌHATU/STONE SOUP —
AN ADAPTED TRADITIONAL EUROPEAN FOLKTALE

This is a very simple story, also sometimes known as 'nail soup'. You can tell it in third person or first person, with yourself as the traveller.

There are a few different ways you can share the story.

1. Simple straightforward narration where the teacher/adult tells the story and the children can suggest the ingredients that the villagers bring and sing the 'chop, chop, chop' song.

2. You could more actively involve the children by asking them to take on the roles of the villagers. Sitting in a circle, the children can be the villagers and you can tell the story from the centre of the circle. You can take turns at knocking on their doors and being turned away and then later they can take turns at being the curious villagers who come in the centre of the circle and offer an ingredient.

I have even told this with real vegetables (and another adult helper – to assist with the chopping, or if the children are older and can safely handle a knife they can do the chopping) with the soup being cooked and shared.

There once was a traveller making his way in the world. Arriving at a village, he knocks on the doors of the people who live there asking if they might give him a place to sleep for the night and something to eat. Nobody is keen to offer hospitality to the man so he makes a fire in the village square and fills a pot he has with water, places a stone in it and puts it on the fire. One by one the villagers' curiosity grew and they came out to enquire.

Villager: "What are you doing?"

Traveller: "I'm making stone soup."

Villager: "You can make soup from a stone? Well who would have guessed!"

Traveller: "Yes it was the King/Queen's *(someone famous/well known to the tamariki)* favourite dish when I used to cook for them. You're welcome to share it with me."

Villager: "I'd love to try some."

Traveller: "Great but you know what? I was just thinking it needs a little more flavour. Would you have a little something you might be willing to add?" *(you can either leave the question open like this or suggest an ingredient).*

The curious villager went back to their house and fetched an (onion), brought it back and it was chopped up and added to the soup. (Each time an ingredient is added this chant can be sung).

Chop, chop, chop, into the pot
Every little bit makes for a lot
Chop, chop, chop, into the pot
We give thanks for what we've got

One by one the curious villagers come out of their homes and each has the same conversation with the traveller. Each one returns home and finds a vegetable or herb that can be added and the soup grows and smells delicious.

Eventually all the villagers have come out into the square and are standing around the fire having contributed an ingredient. The traveller declares the soup ready, takes out the stone and serves up the soup. All those who share the soup declares it's the best soup that they have ever had and the traveller is now considered an honoured guest and given a comfy place to sleep that night.

In the morning, they farewell the traveller who gives them the stone for future soups. They once again declare how amazing stone soup was and the traveller agrees saying, "It always tastes better if everyone adds a little something to it."

STORIES IN THE STARS

Winter is a wonderful time for stargazing. Here in Aotearoa we now have a mid-winter public holiday to celebrate Matariki/Pūanga, the traditional Māori New Year, which is orientated around the return of certain stars/clusters in the winter night sky. Depending on where you are in Aotearoa, this celebration is associated with the first sighting/return of either the Matariki cluster (Pleiades) or the star Pūanga. The Māori New Year celebrations, like many new year celebrations around the world focus on the gathering of whānau/family, sharing of kai, remembering of tūpuna/ancestors, singing and creative activities (in particular the making and flying of kites/manu tukutuku).

There is a growing collection of Matariki resources, songs/stories available online for sharing. I have included some links at the end of these notes. I strongly encourage you to engage with whānau in your school/centre who whakapapa Māori or connect with your local marae to find out how Matariki is/was celebrated in your area and/or connect with wider community celebrations.

Stars are magical things - when we look up at stars we see we are reminded of the origins of our universe and all that we are connected to. Our sun is the closest star to us and is the source of life on our planet. Our movement around the sun gives us day and night and the measure of the year in the Gregorian calendar. Stars have been used by all cultures to mark time and to navigate with. Humans have always told stories about the stars and if you learn to observe the stars you can read the night sky like a book. They are often thought to have auspicious properties as fortune tellers, predicting future events. We also like to cast our wishes upon 'shooting' stars (which are usually meteorites). Looking up at the stars always strikes awe into us and reminds us of the much larger universe that we are part of. The word for star in te reo Māori is whētu.

THE STORYTELLING STAR

Requirements: you will need a star (can be three dimensional, cut out from paper/card, woven from harakeke/flax etc. It needs to be durable enough for tamariki to pass around).

This activity can be introduced with the singing of 'Twinkle, Twinkle Little Star' or a conversation about stars. "I wonder who has looked up at the stars at night?" Or "I wonder what you know about stars?"

Sit the children in a circle. As the song is sung, the star is passed around the circle, when the song stops, the person with the star takes their turn to share what the star can see.

Twinkle, twinkle little star
From up on high you can see far
Looking here and looking there
You can see most everywhere
Twinkle, twinkle shining bright
Tell us what you see tonight

Tirama, tirama ngā whetū
Kei te pēhea ra koutou
Kei runga ake rā

He taimana to rite
Tirama, tirama ngā whetū
Kei te pēhea rā koutou

What the 'star'/child reports, seeing can be extended by questioning.

Child: I see a cow.
Adult: I wonder what the cow is doing?
Child: Sleeping.
Adult: I wonder if cows dream when they sleep, like we do?
Child: I think they do.
Adult: I wonder what cows might dream about?
Child: Flowers and grass.

You may wish to give a short story reflection back to the group: "Indy-Star sees a cow in a field down on the earth. The cow is sleeping and dreaming of flowers and grass."

An alternative to the circle is for tamariki to take turns holding the star (they could stand or sit on a 'viewing chair' while the rest of the group remain seated and sing the song). While the song is being sung the child whose turn it is has time to think about what they/the star might see. When the

song finishes, they can share the 'star's view'. For those children reluctant to stand up alone, they can take their turn with a friend.

THE FALLEN STAR
A PROCESS DRAMA

This is a simple process drama. If you are not familiar with process dramas, please refer to the teaching notes in the appendix. You will need an adult to take on the role of the star (whom we will refer to as TIR – teacher in role) and another adult to facilitate the process (whom we'll call TAF – teacher as facilitator).

Begin by asking the children if they would like to meet a star/or if they have ever met a star? Explain that today instead of reading or telling a story, that the group is going to be the story and they are going to meet a star. Explain that TIR is going to be the star we meet.

"We'll know that she is the star when we meet her because she will be wearing this." 'This' can be a sparkly piece of cloth wrapped like a cloak over the shoulder, a crown (part of the prep could be to make a star crown). You could even ask the tamariki to go and choose/find something uncomplicated that the adult playing the star can wear.

TIR moves to another part of the room where the group can meet her.

When the group approaches TIR she is looking sad. She might be softly crying or sighing.

TAF: "I wonder how the star is feeling?"

Tamariki: "Sad/frightened"

Encourage the children to consider why the star might be sad/frightened etc. and to engage with the TIR and ask questions.

"Are you sad?"

"Is something upsetting you?"

"What's wrong?"

TIR responds, explaining she's fallen out of the sky and bumped her knee or head when she fell.

TAF asks the children what they could do to help. "What do you need when you hurt yourself to help you feel better?"

Children might suggest a hug, a band-aid, a kiss etc.

After the children help the star feel better, the star (TIR) thanks them and tells them her name, Hiwa-i-te-rangi (the wishing star) and that her whānau live in the sky. She is the pōtiki (the youngest in her family). She has to get home because there is going to be an important party/celebration called Matariki/the Māori new year and she has to be there but she doesn't know how she can get back up into the sky. Would the tamariki be able to help her?

The drama now unfolds with the children suggesting how Hiwa (TIR) might get back up into the sky – some of these suggestions can be tried (unsuccessfully as you don't want to solve the challenge immediately)

"Maybe you could do a really big jump back into the sky?"

"Maybe we could get a really long ladder."

"Maybe we can tie lots of balloons to you."

"Maybe an aeroplane."

"Maybe her whānau can come and get her."

"Maybe some birds can give her a ride."

There is no one 'right way' to finish this drama but given the importance of flying manu tukutuku during the celebration of the Māori new year, this idea could certainly be incorporated. The children could make a kite to fly her back to her whānau or Hiwa could become the kite.

But before Hiwa goes she asks the children what their wishes are – after all she is the star of wishes/aspirations for the new year. She will take them back up into the sky and look after them. The star (TIR) has a kete/basket that she collects the wishes into. This can be done as a drawing activity or as a turn taking song. Here is a song you can use:

Recording available

These are my wishes, these are my words
Now they are spoken, I hope they are heard
Then when I am sleeping, all that I need
Shines from the stars and comes to me

The drama is concluded with Hiwa taking her kete of wishes and returning to the sky to her whānau.

MATARIKI RELAXATION
HIWA-I-TE-RANGI,
THE WHETŪ OF WISHING/
DESIRES FOR THE NEW YEAR

Recording available

With this relaxation exercise it helps if you have some music to accompany you – this can be recorded or played live. Dr Hirini Melbourne and Richard Nunns have made some excellent recordings with taonga puoro and there is a relaxation track in the accompanying album.

Ask the tamariki to find a place to lie on their backs on the floor.

I want you all to lie on your backs and close your eyes and make sure your body is not touching anyone else's body. As you breathe in, can you scrunch up your hands, your face and the muscles in your body, so that your body feels all tight and then as you breathe out you can let go and relax your body. (Repeat this three times).

As you are lying there, imagine it is night time and that you are able to see all the stars. There are so many stars - more than you can count. But very early in the morning, down low in the sky is a very special group of stars known as Matariki or sometimes people call them the Pleiades. They are a whānau of stars and always stay together (one by one you can name the stars and what they watch over).

Matariki - is connected to reflection, hope and our connection to the environment

Pōhutukawa – is connected with those who have passed on/died

Waitī – is connected to fresh water and the kai within it

Waitā – is connected to moana and the kai within it

Waipuna-ā-rangi – is connected with the rain

Tupuānuku – is connected to the kai that grows in the soil

Tupuārangi – is connected to sky kai (birds and fruit on trees)

Ururangi – is connected with the winds

Hiwa-i-te-rangi – the youngest, is the wishing star that also ties into our aspirations for the coming year

Let the light of Hiwa-i-te-rangi shine down on you. It shines so brightly, that its light fills up your head, it trickles down your neck and into your chest and out into

your arms, right down into your fingertips.

Your tummy and legs and feet are also filled with light, your whole body is shining bright just like one of the stars. The light makes your body feel light, like it is floating. Hiwa-i-te-rangi is the star of wishes. You can feel it in your heart and send your wishes to Hiwa-i-te-rangi. You might wish for happiness for you and your friends and whānau, or for safety for all animals in the moana – there are many kind things to wish for, this is your special Matariki wish - send your wish to Hiwa-i-te-rangi. Say, "Thank you/ngā mihi Hiwa-i-te-rangi for looking after my wish." Now wiggle your fingers and toes, rock your head from side to side and open your eyes and when you are ready you can quietly sit up.

SPRING — KŌANGA

Ka tangi te wharauroa, ko ngā karere a Mahuru
Māori Whakataukī

If the shining cuckoo cries it is the messenger of Spring
Māori proverb

In the spring, at the end of the day,
you should smell like dirt.
Margaret Atwood

In te ao Māori, kōanga is a time for planting māra/gardens, in particular, kūmara. Kō is a traditional digging garden tool and kō can also mean to sing. Another word for spring in te reo Māori is aroaromahana – facing towards the warmth. The shining cuckoo/Pīpīwharauroa returns to parts of Aotearoa in early spring from wintering over in the Bismarck Archipelago (New Guinea) and Solomon Islands. Her call is tohu/a sign that spring has arrived.

Spring is a time of new beginnings. It's an exciting time! The earth is reinvigorated by the days of increasing light and warmth. Plants start to grow again, often exhibiting new leaves, which we call 'spring growth'. Animals who migrate to warmer places over winter return, their songs heralding the arrival of the season. In general all birds become more vocal as it's time to find a mate, make a nest and lay eggs. Frogs wake up and begin their mating songs (note: native New Zealand frogs idon't sing). It's the time of year to start sowing seeds for a summer garden.

Ironically despite the liveliness of spring, food-wise it can be a lean time. Winter reserves have come to an end and new gardens are not yet established. The aliveness of spring naturally pulls us out of our homes and into the world. It's time to make new plans and begin new projects.

LAYING THE TABLE FOR SPRING

I wonder what the qualities of spring are?

Suggestions: Rebirth, energy, growth, new life, vigour, beginnings

I wonder which plants we usually see in spring?

Suggestions: Kōwhai, native clematis, bulbs (daffodils, tulips etc), kūmara tipu, mānuka, wisteria flowers, oak trees new growth, blossoming fruit trees, flowering kūmarahou, kākā beak/ ngutukākā

I wonder which foods we have available to eat in spring?

Suggestions: Asparagus, broad beans, globe artichokes, leafy greens, spring onions, karengo (seaweed)

I wonder which animals we see in spring?

Suggestions: Pīpīwharauroa (shining cuckoo), tūī, return of the wader birds, hares/rabbits, chickens, baby animals, kererū

I wonder who the atua/deities that can be associated with spring are?

Suggestions: Eostre, Rongomātāne, Pani, the Green Man, Persephone, Flora, Brigid

SPRING SONG
Recording available ♪

Spring, spring the birds do sing
The earth is dressed in green
Spring, spring now plant your seeds
It's time for dreams to grow

Blossoms, bunnies
Bees busy making honey
Kōwhai, kūmara
Pīpīwharauroa

A FOOT STORY

THE TWO GECKOS CELEBRATE SPRING

Please read the notes in the appendix about foot stories. (P 126)

Once upon a time there were two geckos, and when this story started, they were fast asleep, snoring. **Legs stretched out straight in front of the body, toes pointing down to the floor and flexing back towards the chest to the rhythm of the snores.**

When one little gecko woke up and said, "Hooray, what shall we do today." **Lift your right leg and shake.** He tried to wake up his friend, "Wake up! Wakeup!" **Tap left leg with right leg.**

But his friend was fast asleep, so the little gecko went and fetched an alarm clock. **Left leg continues to point and flex. Right leg bends and tip toes out to the side, level with the hip and returns to front centre. Both legs stretched out straight in front of the body.**

The alarm clock went, "Brrrrrrring." But the little gecko still slept. *Shake your whole body gently.*

So the alarm clock rang louder, "Brrrring." But still the gecko slept. **Shake the whole body a little more vigorously.**

So the alarm clock rang as loud as it could, "Brrrrring." **Shake your whole body with force.**

And the little gecko jumped up, "Hooray!" **Lift your left foot into the air and return to the floor.**

"Hooray!" said her friend. "What shall we do today?" **Turn feet towards each other, and wriggle each foot in turn as it speaks.**

"Let's go outside and play. But first, let's do our exercises." So the two little geckos went point and flex and point and flex. **Point and flex feet.**

Round and around and around and around and then the other way. **Ankle rotations (turn feet in small circles from the ankle) of both feet in both directions.**

Then in and out and in and out and in and out. **In a sitting position jump feet apart and then back together again three times.**

And then off they set. They went walk, walk, walk, walk. Skippity-hop, skippity-hop, jump, jump, jump, jump. Stop! (x3) **Rhythm of different steps performed using the feet in a sitting position, with bent knees.**

There in front of them was a pond. **Place soles of feet together and open legs into a diamond shape.** There sitting on a rock on the edge of the pond was a frog with big googly eyes **fingers around eyes,** large sticky feet **place hands flat on either side of the body** and strong, strong legs **kick legs out in front while seated.**

The two little geckos tried to creep up on the frog. They went creep, creep, creep but the frog jumped and splashed into the safety of the pond.

From a sitting knees-bent position, creep the feet forwards and with the jump, stretch the hands out towards the feet.

Then there on a lily pad they saw another frog. They went creep, creep, creep but the frog jumped and splashed into the safety of the pond. **From a sitting knees-bent position, creep the feet forwards and with the jump, stretch the hands out towards the feet.**

But then hidden in the harakeke was a third frog. They went creep, creep, creep but the frog jumped and splashed into the safety of the pond. **From a sitting knees-bent position, creep the feet forwards and with the jump, stretch the hands out towards the feet.**

All the frogs were now hidden in the pond and so the geckos continued on their way. They went walk, walk, walk, walk. Skippity-hop, skippity-hop, jump, jump, jump, jump. Stop! (x3) **Rhythm of different steps performed using the feet in a sitting position, with bent knees.**

All of a sudden they heard a sound. Bzzzzzz. It was a bee. **Seated position with feet pressed together making a diamond shape, legs bouncing/flapping like a bee.**

The geckos followed the bee and it came to a tall, tall flower. It stretched into the flower, this way and that way with its long proboscis and sucked up the nectar. Yum, Yum. **Stretch arms straight up over head, stretch to one side and then the other and rub your tummy for yum, yum.**

The bee flew to another tall, tall flower. It stretched into the flower, this way and that way with its long proboscis and sucked up the nectar. Yum, Yum. **Stretch arms straight up overhead, stretch to one side and then the other and rub your tummy for yum, yum.**

And then the bee flew to another tall, tall flower. It stretched into the flower, this way and that way with its long proboscis and sucked up the nectar. Yum, Yum - and then it flew back to the hive. **Stretch arms straight up over head, stretch to one side and then the other and rub your tummy for yum, yum.**

And so the geckos continued on their way. They went walk, walk, walk, walk. Skippity-hop, skippity-hop, jump, jump, jump, jump. Stop! (x3) **Rhythm of different steps performed using the feet in a sitting position, with bent knees.**

There in front of them was a great big kōwhai tree all covered in golden yellow blossom. **Lie on back and lift legs straight up into the air, stretch out arms for 'all covered in blossom'.**

When who should come flying past but a big, fat kererū. **Roll back up onto your bottom and flap arms.**

The kererū landed on a branch and the branch went bend, then on another branch and the branch went bend. **Roll back onto back with legs extended above, lean right leg to the right and then the left leg. Do this on each side three times with the branches bending.**

And then the kererū flew away. There, under the tree was a little brown shell. When the geckos looked more closely they saw something slowly coming out from the shell. It was a snail. **Curl into 'pose of the child' with arms by the side; as the snail creeps out from the shell, bring the arms forward and wiggle the fingers, then pull quickly back to resting posture again. Repeat three times.**

The geckos waited but the snail stayed hidden in its shell. And so the geckos headed back home. They went walk, walk, walk, walk. Skippity-hop, skippity-hop, jump, jump, jump, jump. Stop! (x3). And when they got home, they jumped into bed and fell fast asleep, listening to the sounds of the frogs singing.

EGG–CITING STORIES FOR SPRING

Many people often fail to make the connection between eggs and spring probably because we celebrate Easter (the northern spring festival) in Australia and New Zealand in Autumn. If you are lucky enough to have the company of a few chickens, that connection will come as no surprise to you, but for many of us, our eggs (if you eat them) come from shops and shops always have eggs regardless of the season.

Chickens do not naturally lay eggs all year round. Their rate of laying is stimulated by light (length of the days) and warmth and of course we have meddled with their genes to breed hens who lay much more frequently than their wild relatives, jungle fowl. The seasonal increase of these two factors, light and warmth, indicate to many animals that it's now a safe time to have their offspring (of spring). The warmer weather increases the likelihood that new-borns will live and that there will be food to feed them.

The egg in many cultures is the symbol of life and rebirth. Even humans started our journey as a fertilised egg in the nest/the womb of our mothers. The egg essentially is the animal equivalent of a seed.

In the northern hemisphere eggs were gifted, painted/decorated and preserved in spring because there was such an abundance of them. So now is the time to do all those fun traditional egg decorating, hunting and gifting activities not in Autumn when the calendar Easter falls. March/April/May are our times of harvesting summer's abundance.

STORYTELLING EGGS

Over the years I have collected together all manner of decorated 'eggs' from around the world. Wooden, felted, brass, beaded, glass and sometimes even hand blown eggs, which are extremely fragile. You might like to start your own 'story egg' collection. It's a great device for stimulating storytelling or for using as a framing device, even when it's not springtime.

Alternatively you can do egg decorating with children. I encourage you to try and source eggs locally or buy certified free-range eggs. With younger children I suggest boiled egg decorating and with older children you might want to try blowing eggs but a word of warning – you'll have very sore jowls afterwards – it takes quite a bit of puff to blow an egg. You can cook up the egg content you blow out in baking or scrambled eggs to share.

OSTEREIERBAUM

The Ostereierbaum or Easter tree – is an old German tradition. These can be created indoors or outdoors – much like a Christmas Tree, only the tree is decorated with eggs. A bare branch makes for a good indoor Ostereierbaum or outdoors, a living tree that is small enough so that the children can reach the branches. It's pretty difficult to hang a boiled egg in a tree and so I suggest weaving a little basket from paper or flax to hold the egg and then hang the basket in the tree.

GUIDED VISUALISATION FOR USING WITH STORY EGGS

Recording available

You may wish to use some relaxation music with this activity playing quietly in the background. To begin the exercise, encourage the children to find a place to lie down on their backs (if there is enough room) or to just close their eyes where they are sitting. Take them through a cycle of three deep breaths (or more if needed) to bring their attention to their breath and help them relax. Begin to tell the story.

Can you imagine a huge mountain, stretching up towards the sky? Go to the top of that mountain and you will find a stream flowing down the mountain. Follow that stream until you reach the ocean. There waiting for you on the shore is a boat, climb aboard and sail out across the ocean until you reach an island. Land your boat on the shore and there ahead of you, you'll see a path. Follow that path into the forest until you come to a clearing. There stands a huge tree and in its branches is a nest. Climb the tree and look into the nest and you will find the story eggs. *(Ask the children to slowly sit up and open their eyes.)* If you take an egg and listen well, inside each egg is a story to tell.

From this point either you choose an egg from the nest or off the tree to begin your story. Alternatively ask a child to do the selecting. You may have a story associated with the egg you have chosen or if the child has chosen an egg, ask them what kind of story they think might be in the egg. From here you can either lead the story or work with the child/children to create a story using the suggestions from the child who chose the egg.

MAKING NESTS

A story nest is an evocative place to share stories, a cosy den of creativity where ideas can hatch. You can build a story nest inside or outside.

Begin with a conversation about nest building. Perhaps you have access to an old nest from last spring to begin the conversation, or you could share one of any number of picture books that focus on nests or the song 'I'm a little Bird' as shared later in this chapter. Find out what the children already know and have experienced when it comes to nests.

Before you begin, it is good to be clear with the group whether you are making a literal nest or an imaginative nest. Children's natural inclination in my experience is to collect physical items such as cushions, blankets, sticks, clothes etc. If you have an agreement about the task to hand before you begin, expectations are more likely to be met. With an imaginative nest you are not restricted by what is physically available to build the nest with.

Start by sitting with the tamariki in a circle on the floor. Explain that we are going to gather things/ideas to build a nest in the centre of the circle. Children can take turns individually or work in pairs to collect while the song is being sung.

NEST BUILDING SONG

Recording available ♪

(*Child/children's names*) **flies high**
(*Child/children's names*) **flies low**
(*Child/children's names*) **flies around the world
round and round they go**
(*Child/children's names*) **flies slow**
(*Child/children's names*) **flies fast**
What has/have (*Child/children's names*) **found
to build a nest for us**

The child/children skip around the group seated in a circle while the song is sung. At the end of the song they enter the circle and share what they have found/imagined to contribute to making a nest. This contribution can be extended with questioning:

- **I wonder where you found that?**
- **I wonder if that was difficult to find?**
- **I wonder why that would be good for building a nest?**

Repeat until everyone who wants to has had at least one turn. If you have a physical nest (depending on its size) you can come and inhabit your nest. If it is an imaginative nest you can describe what the children have created to them and perhaps pose the question: "I wonder if anyone might come and lay some eggs in this nest?"

This can be a 'springboard' for all kinds of interesting conversations, story making/sharing activities.

CONCERT TODAY!

You can create a story about the nest and what happens in it, or if you have built a larger nest that is big enough to accommodate people, then it can be a place where storytelling and sharing can take place. This can be as simple as leaving some picture books in the nest for the children to enjoy.

I'M A LITTLE BIRD

by Helen Willberg

Recording available ♪

I'm a little bird
And I'm hatching from my shell
Out pops my head
My tail as well
Now my legs I stretch
And now my wings I flap
I fly around, I fly around
Now what do you think of that?
Down, down, down, down, down, down,
                        down, down

This is sung to an ascending then descending scale. Each line or 'down' is sung on a note (eight notes in a scale). Children begin curled up on the floor/in the nest and move through the actions as they are sung, until they are standing and flying around the room. On the descending scale they return back to the nest/floor. This can be extended into a story-making exercise through open ended questioning:

* I wonder what kind of bird you'll hatch into?
* I wonder what you saw when you were flying around?
* I wonder if you brought anything back to the nest with you?

THE BIRD WHO LOST HER SONG

A PROCESS DRAMA

If you are unfamiliar with process dramas, please see the introduction to this wonderful form of story exploration in the appendix. (P 117)

TAF refers to 'teacher as facilitator'.
TIR refers to 'teacher in role'.

Beginning the drama

Gather a group into a seated circle. Explain to them that instead of telling/reading a story, today we are going to 'be the story.' We are going to be the characters in the story and decide what happens.

Introducing the provocation — an invitation (a letter)

To help create focus on the task, you could use the 'story box' and the following song. A 'story box' is any vessel that conceals what you are going to share. This is a useful device for younger children. Alternatively, you could have another adult deliver the letter to the group - as themselves or as the postie.

Recording available

Here is the story box
Here is its lid
I wonder what inside is hid
Is it a (woof, woof) dog?
Or maybe a (baa, baa) sheep
Maybe it's just a smelly old sock
Shall we count to three and see
what we've got
One, two, three

Open the box and take the letter out to share. Either read the letter to the children, or if there are confident readers in the group encourage them to read the letter.

Dear Tamariki/Children

I am writing to invite you to my singing
concert to hear my new song.
I hope you can come.
Please come to the big tree today.
Kind wishes

Tūī/Magpie (songbird of your choice)

Discuss the invitation with the children.

- **How exciting – I wonder if any of you have been to a concert before?**
- **I wonder what the new song might be about.**
- **I'm really excited. I've never been to a concert before!**
- **The big tree! I wonder where that might be?**
- **I wonder if we need to take anything with us.**

Making the journey

Depending on your group, time constraints, and how the children respond, the next part of the drama may involve movement, planning/drawing or narrating.

Example:

Child/children: "I know the way to the big tree."

TAF: "That's great, maybe we can draw some maps."

Get out paper/pencils and create some maps.

Child/children: "The big tree is far away."

TAF: "I wonder how we might get there?"

Child/children: "Walk. Ride our bicycles. Catch a bus."

These ideas can be narrated or moved and sung using a song:

Recording available ♪

We are going to a big, big tree
It's a long, long way to go
I wonder how we'll get there?
Maybe somebody knows

From what the children suggest, as the storyteller, narrate the journey that the group made. Example: "We were all so excited to receive an invitation to a concert. Shelby and Lucas had been to a concert before and told us we had to be very good at listening and that sometimes you can have an ice cream. So, we took our best listening ears and caught a bus to the big tree."

Meeting the bird
adult in role/puppet

Once you have arrived at the 'big tree', explain to the children that we're now going to meet the bird who has invited us to the concert.

The bird can be played by yourself/another adult (TIR)/puppet. If the role is played by another adult/yourself then have a simple prop that you can wear to signal your change into character (e.g. a feather boa/ half bird mask/hat). Talk the children through the process:

"Do you ever dress up and imagine you are someone different? In today's story, I am going to play the bird who sent us the invitation. I have this feathery hat and when I put it on, I won't be Tanya anymore, I'll be the bird. I might use a different voice. I'm going to sit on that chair over there and put the boa/mask/hat on and you can come and find me. I wonder how the bird might be feeling about the concert?"

Introducing the problem

When the children meet the bird, she is sad. She tells the children that she has lost her new song. She was out flying, and it fell out of her mouth. So now there can be no concert. She doesn't need to blurt this all out at once – it is important for the children to build a relationship. Here are some ideas about how to proceed:

1. **Bird/Tūī is crying when the children meet her. Children enquire about why the bird is crying. If using a puppet or another adult – you can help facilitate the interaction, "I wonder why Tūī is crying?"**

2. **Tūī greets the children and asks if they have come for the concert. When the children say they have, she apologises and says she has had to cancel the concert. Children can ask - why?**

3. **When the children arrive, Bird is hunting for something muttering, "Where can it be? I can't find it anywhere." Group can enquire: "What are you looking for?"**

SOLVING THE PROBLEM

In my experience, children generally want to help when they witness someone distressed. While we want to engage their assistance/interaction, we don't want to make the problem too easy to solve. We want to positively and creatively 'frustrate' them in their problem solving.

A child might say, "I found your song." And hand 'the song' to the bird.

TIR as bird could respond by swallowing the

song and making a sound that is not hers, like hooting or crowing. "I think that might be an owl's or a rooster's song. That's not my song."

Possible responses

TAF: "I wonder what Tūī's song looks/sounds like?"

TIR: "It's got high bits and low bits, quiet bits and loud bits and round and round bits."

Encourage children to move their bodies to the description given or draw a song.

Children could teach Tūī/bird a new song that they all know.

Child: "I know a song - happy birthday."

Children could go on a hunt to find Tūī's song.

TAF: "Let's all go and have a look and see if we can find Tui's song."

If children return with lots of 'songs' Tūī/Bird can try the different songs.

She may or may not find her song amongst them.

TAF: "Maybe we could make you a new song?"

As a group children work to create a new song for Tūī/bird – again this would involve a discussion about what a song is, what a song is made of (I wonder if it's a happy song, fast, about flowers? etc.). This can be drawn or moved.

Song Making Circle

Move into a circle formation with the group. Ask the tamariki for ingredients (a bit like making a cake). Children can take turns suggesting ideas and the other children can respond by copying or giving an action/sound to the suggestion.

Conclusion

TIR sings her song (either a new song or the song found). Children can sing with her or offer her a 'thank you' song in response. TIR thanks the children for helping her and saving/coming to the concert.

The TIR then comes out of role and the drama concludes: "Thank you for all your help today. We're going to finish our story now."

IN THE GARDEN
A CUMULATIVE STORY
FOR SPRING

Spring is a busy time in the garden. It's a great time to sow seeds after the resting period of winter. I created this story as a keen gardener. It uses a very simple story structure where each time the narrative is repeated a new character, item, or challenge is added. These are known as cumulative tales (or sometimes called a chain or add-on stories) and are very popular story forms to use with young children. Well-known cumulative folktales you might be familiar with are:

- **The Gingerbread Man**
- **Chicken Licken**
- **The Giant Turnip**
- **This the House that Jack Built**

I often start this story by introducing seeds to the children. If you choose to do this please use edible/organic seeds as many commercial seeds are coated in toxic fungicide and children may want to touch the seeds.

To introduce the seeds, you could use the 'story box' idea from the previous section to help create suspense and focus. Once the seeds are introduced, begin telling the story. You can either tell this story in the first person (as yourself) or in the third person (about someone else).

Recording available

It's spring! Time to plant seeds in the garden. So I collected my seeds, ready to plant, so I would have lots of delicious vegetables to eat. Into the garden shed I went to collect my spade to dig the soil. But when I went to dig the soil, the spade was blunt.

"Spade, spade, why won't you dig?" I asked.

"I need to be sharpened," said the spade.

So, I went and got the sharpening stone, to sharpen the spade. But the stone would not sharpen the spade.

"Stone, stone, why won't you sharpen the spade, so I can dig the soil and plant my seeds, so I'll have lots of delicious vegetables to eat?"

"I need water splashed on me to sharpen the spade."

So, I went and got a bucket to fetch some water, but when I filled the bucket with water it all ran out through a hole.

"Bucket, bucket – why won't you hold the water, so I can wet the stone, so the stone can sharpen the spade, so I can dig the soil, to plant my seeds so I have lots of delicious vegetables to eat?"

"I have a hole," said bucket. "You need to fill it with some mud/clay."

So, I went to fetch some mud/clay from a sticky puddle, but the puddle was very sticky, and I got stuck.

"Puddle, puddle, unstick me! I need some mud to fill the hole in the bucket so I can carry water to the stone, to sharpen the spade, so I can dig the soil and plant my seeds and have lots of delicious vegetables to eat."

"You need a log to stand on, so you won't get stuck," said the puddle.

And so, I went and found a log but under that log was a frog.

"What are you doing?" said the frog.

"Oh frog, I need a log, so I won't get stuck, when I collect the mud, to fill the hole in the bucket, so I can carry the water to the stone to sharpen the spade, so I can dig the soil and plant my seeds and have lots of delicious vegetables to eat."

"I see," said the frog. "Well, if you caught me a fly, I would give you this log."

And so, I went to catch a fly. But catching flies is tricky and you have to be sneaky, and you have to be fast.

I went – creep, creep, creep, and snatch – no fly.

I went – creep, creep, creep, and snatch – no fly.

I went – creep, creep, creep, and snatch – and buzz.

I caught a fly.

I gave the fly to the frog, who went hippity hoppity from under the log. I took the log and put it over the puddle. I stepped on the log and collected the mud. I fixed the hole in the bucket and filled it with water. I carried the water to the stone. I wet the stone and sharpened the spade and dug the soil and planted my seeds and they grew, and they grew, and they grew, and I had lots of delicious vegetables to eat.

I wonder what kind of vegetables I grew?

Cumulative tales are great story forms for strengthening memory. Remembering the narrative is easier if you give an action to each item in the story.

Example: Digging action for spade, fist for the stone, circled arms for the bucket.

After repeating the narrative a few times, pause for children to 'fill in the gaps' with either actions or words.

Example: "Oh frog, I need a log, so I won't get ___ when I collect the ___, to fill the ___ in the ___, so I can carry the ___, to the ___ to sharpen the ___, so I can ___ the ___ and ___ my ___ and have lots of ___"

VARIATIONS

When the tamariki become confident with the narrative, you can ask individuals to take on the roles of the various objects/characters and to help you tell the story. With older children the story can also be passed around the circle with people taking turns to tell different parts of the story.

GUIDED MASSAGE
SEED MASSAGE

Ask the children to find a partner. One child will give the massage and the other is the recipient of the massage, or the seed. Always stress to children the importance of respecting another person's body. Discourage children from touching another person's head.

If the person receiving the massage asks the person giving the massage to stop, the massage must stop. You can get the children to practise massage actions on their own thigh to begin with, so they can have a sense of the strength of their own touch. The massage actions are performed using the hands lightly, on the back of the child who is curled up, knees and head on the floor, back pointing to the ceiling.

SEED MASSAGE SONG

Recording available ♪

Into the moist, dark earth we carefully
                    plant the seeds
Pat, pat, pat
Pat, pat, pat
Pat, pat, pat
There they lie, still and sleeping, waiting
                    to grow

The sun shines and strokes the earth
Glowing and warm
Glowing and warm
Glowing and warm

The rain sings its watery gifts
Pitter, patter, plop
Pitter, patter, plop
Pitter, patter, plop

The air whispers
Wake up
Wake up
Wake up

And the seed begins to move
They wriggle and open and begin to grow

Out of the ground they sprout
Green leaves forming, reaching towards
                                the sun
Roots threading and pushing through
                                the earth

Bigger and bigger
Stronger and stronger
Taller and taller

Now the seed is a plant
I wonder what kind of plant has grown
                        from this seed?

GRATITUDE AND REFLECTION

We can plant seeds, like intentions. Pose the question to the tamariki:

"I wonder what you would like to see more of growing in the world?"

APPENDIX

Notes on process drama

(excerpt from Imagined Worlds – a journey through the expressive arts in early childhood by Tanya Batt)

The arts are powerful forms of personal and social expression. They link imagination, thinking and feeling. They provide essential learning for living and develop a wide range of both general and specific skills that are significant in many aspects of life. They encourage the growth of self-knowledge and self-worth. They encourage students to investigate their own values and those of others, and to recognise the aesthetic and spiritual dimensions of their lives.

The process dramas in this resource are strongly influenced by the work of Dorothy Heathcote and the later elaboration of her work by people such as Kathleen Warren. Practitioners of process drama advocate an approach that builds upon children's own experiences and interests, and views drama as a means by which children can come to understand the world that they live in. There is no external audience. The elements of 'theatre' are utilised to promote self-understanding and to aid enquiry. The experiences are then crystalized through the processes of reflection and evaluation.

Process drama is a highly interactive medium. Children interact with their peers, the adults involved, the fictional context, and their environment. There are opportunities to express and trial their own ideas, and to listen and respect the ideas of others; times to work individually and tasks that require co-operative team work. Adults provide support, encouragement and challenges to the children's endeavours, as well as facilitating opportunities for the children to give direction to the drama and to experience the consequences of their decisions.

Defining terms

TAF - Teacher as Facilitator

For reasons of brevity the abbreviation TAF will be used in this resource to refer to the adults working to facilitate the drama. The TAF has a special role in the drama and her tasks are considerable and varied. They will introduce the fictional context and help the children identify, clarify and discuss the issue at hand. They are there as both a mediator to the children's ideas and the interactions between the TIR and the children. They may both support the children or play the devil's advocate. Their skill is in questioning, and encouraging focus and commitment to the task at hand. They can be the midwife of children's understanding and expression.

TIR - Teacher in role

TIR, refers to the adult taking on a character (e.g. bird, star etc) in the course of presenting the drama. Ideally two adults are required for most dramas though it is possible for the TAF to become the TIR, or for the character to be played by a puppet. Two adults allow one adult to work with the group as the TAF and the other to take on the roles. The purpose of this role will vary with different dramas. The nature of the role will serve to elicit different responses from the children. The TIR may take on a role of high status, which will give them authority to challenge or support the children, such as a queen; or one of low status, such as a person, who requires the children's assistance, such as Jill who has lost her bucket. Other times the function of their role will be to introduce material central to the drama or to encourage through enquiry, the children's own reasoning and reflection. Ideally, in a drama, there is a shifting and sharing of power. Drama is not about adults maintaining all the power. Therefore the TIR needs to be carefully considered.

Presenting a drama experience – practicalities

Choose a suitable environment

If you are working in an early childhood centre, try to minimise possible distractions in order to give children the best possible opportunities to concentrate. You may have the option of using a separate room or area, away from the main activity of the centre. In a school you may have the use of a music or drama room. Small children rattle around in large halls and I would recommend a smaller more intimate space rather than a large, gaping hall.

Think about your use of space

When planning a drama, think about how you will use the physical space in order to help structure and contain the drama. Is there enough room to physically travel? Where will the children meet the TIR? Will the TIR be on the floor or a chair? How many different imaginary locations might there be in the drama, and where will these take place in the room? Do we need to be able to display pictures, maps etc that the children have drawn? Is the surface of the floor suitable for drawing upon?

These may seem like miniscule details, but it is surprising how often the success of a drama can be undermined by poor organisational planning. I speak from experience, having presented the same drama four times in a day in four different physical spaces. Children feel frustrated when their drawing materials penetrate and rip the paper on which they are trying to record their ideas, and irritable when they don't have space to move or aren't able to see what is happening. Planning carefully enables you to spend more time focused on the drama and less time dealing with behavioural difficulties arising from poor organisation.

Group size

Think carefully about the number of children you want to work with. Some people will advocate that you simply work with whatever number of children you have. In some cases you may find that you have little choice. In other cases we simply assume that we have little choice. Quality learning opportunities are worth fighting for, and I would much rather present a successful drama experience to smaller group, where the adult to child ratio was such that I was able to engage the attention of and listen to the contributions made by all children than to present the same session to a larger group, where I was unable to adequately respond to the group's needs. With three to four-year-olds, I ideally like groups of ten children, with a maximum of fifteen. That is not to say that drama sessions cannot take place with much larger groups.

How many adults?

Ideally most process dramas work best with two adults, one to facilitate the drama and the other to take on the roles. Puppets can be used for role work.

General principles in presenting drama to young children

It can be helpful having some kind of frame or guideline when going about the planning of a drama. It can help make clear what ingredients and techniques make for a successful session. Different drama practitioners will have different approaches. Kathleen Warren in her book, *Hooked on Drama: the Theory and Practice of Drama in Early Childhood*, summarises eight general principles to keep in mind when planning drama experiences for young children. These may be useful to refer to as an additional guide. Not all the dramas in this book follow this exact sequence nor should these principles be considered prescriptive.

Choosing a focus

In choosing a focus it is important to identify both the 'dramatic' potential, and what you hope that children might gain from the experience. There is no drama unless there is tension – a problem that needs solving. In presenting drama to children, one must plan carefully. It is important to consider what responses children are likely to make once the problem is introduced. Of course children may come up with ideas that you have not considered. The more carefully you plan and the clearer you are in terms of your own objectives, the easier it is to deviate from your plan and incorporate the children's own suggestions and interests.

Introducing and agreeing upon the fictional context

Drama is about working in a fictional or imagined experience. It is important that the group has agreed to enter the fictional context. When seeking to explain an imaginary context to young children, I often draw upon their own experiences of imaginary play. "Do you ever dress up and imagine that you are somebody different?" In this context, drama is not about 'tricking' an audience, for we are all colluding participants. The dramatic tools that we use, such as TIR, are transparent, and children witness and instruct adults as they make the transition from TAF, into that of queen or farmer. When a child challenges the fictional context (ie, "that's not really a dragon, that's my mum."), the TAF can agree with the child but gently remind them that for now we have all agreed to take part in the drama and that their mother is taking on the role of a dragon in the drama.

Creating a collective pool of ideas

This is a discussion time in which the TAF has the opportunity to discuss with the children the general topic and at times, specifics of the drama that is about to ensue. It is an opportunity for the children to share their experiences and knowledge of the given subject. It may take place either before going into the role or after going into the role.

Example: In introducing the drama of Mrs Wash-a-lot to the children, I ask about their own experiences with washing, whether that be washing themselves, the dishes, cars, toys, or helping with the laundry. In the course of this discussion all sorts of information comes to the fore.

- Machines that help us wash: dishwashers, washing machines, hoses etc

- Washing essentials: water, soap, washing powder
- Actions associated with washing: scrubbing, spinning, squeezing etc

Later in the drama, Mrs Wash-a-lot can enquire about the children's experiences in washing, (she wishes to be sure of their competence), enabling the children to demonstrate their knowledge, builds both their confidence and their commitment to the drama.

These discussions also allow the TAF to assess the depth of the children's own knowledge, define any key terms or concepts, to pool ideas and to gather material that has come from the children's own experiences that can then later be introduced into the drama. From this point, the TAF is credibly able to acknowledge the children as people who know about washing or farms and then invite them to take a role appropriate to the subject chosen.

Taking on roles

In this kind of drama it is usual for both the adults involved and the children to take on roles.

The children taking on roles

It is important to get children's agreement to take on roles. The TAF might say, "You seem to be people who know a lot about farms, I know a farmer who needs some help on her farm. Would you be willing to take on the role of farm hands in today's drama?"

Children can also operate in a drama as themselves. Roles for children are nearly always group roles, i.e. farm hands, assistant bird collectors, guards etc. Young children tend not to take individual roles, for reasons of practicality i.e. group management and consideration for both the individual child and the group's wellbeing. The purpose of a TIR is both to extend and respond to the children's suggestions. Young children are just learning about their own needs. Their own needs and agenda are in danger of dominating the drama and they are not always able to respond in a thought provoking manner to the varying needs of a group.

That is not to say that I have never had children take individual roles. This happened once in a drama based on the story of Māui and the Sun, where the children were in the role of villagers, who are frustrated by the speed at which the sun travels across the sky. The villagers come together to find a solution to slow the sun. It so transpired that the children thought that the best plan would be to go and talk to the moon, who might be in a better position to talk to the sun. The children didn't think that the sun would listen to them. Travelling in a rocket to the moon, one of the older four years olds in the group insisted on taking the role of the moon. She spoke with great dignity and authority and instructed the children to make gifts for the sun, in order to persuade him to slow his passage. If children do take on key individual roles then the TAF must be prepared to respond to the ideas or direction the child in the role offers.

However, on the whole, this occurrence is the exception rather than the rule. Often the prospect of taking a role is more appealing than the actual act. When given the chance children often melt under the attention of the group, feeling vulnerable and shy.

Because the children are often directing the TIR, they are in effect managing the characteristics of the individual roles. For example, in a drama where the children journey to find a dragon and its treasure, in the hope that the dragon might give them some of his ill-gotten gains, the children discuss and decide upon the characteristics and the nature of the dragon before encountering the TAF in role as the dragon.

Introducing the Teacher in Role (TIR)

TIR is not about an adult making his/her award winning performance. Teachers and parents do not have to be actors to do role work with children. Adults who have skills in this area can bring a richness to a role. Alternatively, over acting or 'hamming it up' can often be counterproductive to the drama. When the children are reduced to giggles or tears or are so absorbed in the adult's performance they often forget about their own roles.

With young children it is important for the role transition to take place in front of the children. This is especially important when you first start working with a group or when the TIR is playing a character that the children perceive as threatening or scary. Introduce the person out-of-role beforehand, ie "Daniel's mum," or "your teacher, Dale, is going to take on the role of our dragon in our drama today." Take time to discuss with the children the characteristics of the TIR.

Example: A group of children receive a notice, asking for crew for an around the world adventure. They immediately pick up on the symbols of the skull and crossbones, which illustrate the notice. They suppose that the notice is from a pirate. The TAF can then ask them what they know about pirates, and then later if they would like to meet the pirate that wrote this notice. The group can then take what they know about pirates and use it to create the pirate they are going to meet. Finally with the children's agreement, the TAF can explain that she is going to put some different clothes on, (showing these to the children) and when she comes back she won't be the 'teacher' anymore, she'll be playing the part of the pirate.

Alternatively, explain that another adult will be taking on the role. The TAF can also stress that if they are unsure about the Pirate, then they could tell them and they could come out of the role and be the 'teacher' again. This transition can be practised as often as necessary.

Keep the costume simple. This both enables you to move quickly and easily in and out of role and fosters a symbolic reading of the role. A scarf or hat may be all that is necessary to denote the character. Keep your face clear. The use of full-face masks with young children is not recommended. Half-face masks can be worn on the forehead so that the eyes and face are still fully visible.

Preparing children to meet TIR

Once the TIR is ready, it can be useful to discuss with children what they might expect when meeting the TIR and what responses they might make to the TIR in role. "What do you think the queen might say to us? How will we speak to a queen?"

In the course of engaging with a TIR, children may well feel angry, frightened, sad or happy. We learn through emotional experiences. However, there is little use in a child being so distressed by the TIR, that he or she is unable to participate.

When children express their anticipation of fear at the prospect of meeting a character of dubious repute (ie dragon, troll, pirate), again discuss with the group why they might feel afraid and what we can do to keep ourselves safe. Give some examples – e.g. going with a friend, taking a magic protective charm with us, or coming up with a plan – should the character prove to be unfriendly. Sometimes children want to take a weapon with them, although I acknowledge the subtext, which is "I am afraid and this is how I choose to feel safe", I personally discourage the use of weapons, through either posing the suggestion to the group, "What do you think about taking a gun into the jungle?" Children peers are often much more effective dissuaders, usually on the grounds that we might accidentally hurt someone, "What if we accidentally shot someone?" You could also use the drama to legitimise a decision: "The part of the jungle we are going into is a National Park and all the animals are protected."

It is important for the children to develop both belief and an affinity for the TIR, otherwise they have not 'invested' in the drama and have little reason to commit to finding a solution.

Presenting the problem

Often the TIR works to either present a problem to the children that requires solving, or presents an obstacle or attitude that prevents the children from reaching a solution. The TIR task is to challenge and extend the children's thinking. When children meet distressed or sad characters, their natural response is to try and find immediate solutions. The immediate solving of problems – ie finding Jill's bucket that has been stolen by a magpie, would not work to develop dramatic tension, quite the opposite, the tension which has been driving the drama dissolves. Drama is not simply about solving problems, it is about the journey we take in arriving at that solution. Elicit explanations and possible solutions from the children.

Questioning plays a very important role in drama. Finding the most effective questions is perhaps that greatest challenge for both the TAF and the TIR. The most productive form of questioning is that which aids children's own enquiry and encourages them to reflect upon their suggestions and choices.

The framing of our questions is also very important. Children quickly learn that they are rewarded for giving the 'right' answer. If children think that the TAF already has an answer in mind, they will direct their efforts at guessing the "right answer," rather than creatively considering a solution to a problem.

For example, in the drama of the Dirty House the children are asked to consider who might dwell in the 'dirty house'. If the TAF were simply to ask directly, "Who lives in the house?" It may sound to the children very much like the TAF already knows who lives in the house. By simply adding the words, "I wonder who might live in this house?" suggests that the TAF does not necessarily know and is inviting the children to speculate.

The TAF should not necessarily act upon the first responses that the children make. Suggestions can be acknowledged and considered. All possible solutions should be heard. Encourage children to consider and respond to other children's suggestions, and to give reasons for their own suggestions. The TIR can respond to children's suggestions by presenting further questions or obstacles. The children might suggest that Jill should simply get a new bucket. The TIR as Jill could respond that the bucket was a favourite one. The children might suggest that they should cut all the trees down on a farm, so the birds eating the farmer's cabbages would have nowhere to live. The TIR could ask, "What about the other animals on the farm who enjoy and need the trees?" Various ideas can be discussed and tried. When a suitable number of ideas have been canvassed or trialled, choices which are to be accepted can be verbally cued by the adult facilitating, to the TIR: the children say they could climb the tree and fetch the bucket, and the drama can proceed.

Acting upon choices and following through with consequences

The decision to fetch Jill's bucket involves climbing the tree and the decision to fetch the golden box involves making a journey. Every choice has a consequence, which in turn throws up its own series of challenges. It is the TAF's responsibility to employ an appropriate teaching strategy that both enables and challenges the children's choices. These might include: drawing pictures, map making, rituals, creating a dance, an action song, creating still images. The purpose of those teaching strategies may be:

- Preparation – In the Bird Collector, the children must prepare themselves for a journey into the jungle.

- Collection – in the Dragon's Birthday, the children work to collect ingredients that they think would make a sick dragon well.

- Bargaining – in the Golden Box, the children exchange their 'B' objects with the troll for the golden box.

- Instructing – in Mrs Wash-a-lot and the Wind, the children teach the wind to blow gently.

Often dramas involve children making journeys. Journeys often provide an opportunity for children to physically move. This can be desirable, especially if children have been sitting for sometime in discussion. Here are a number of different teaching strategies that you might employ in taking a journey:

- You may wish to sing a preparation song. Example: 'We're going on a journey today.'

- You may wish to story tell. Example: Create the journey as a shared story that is created by the group.

- You may wish to do a guided movement exploration. Example: Using a piece of music, interpret the music in making a journey. A quick tempo, may invoke darting and running, slower music - sliding. The TAF guides and challenges children's movement. "The wind has picked you up and you are turning and twisting through the clouds. What speed or level can you turn? How many ways can you twist your body?"

- You may wish to sing an action song. Example: 'Going to Wellington' by Rae Storey.

- You may wish to draw maps.

- You may wish to negotiate and build a structure. Example: The children might decide to travel to the jungle in a bus or aeroplane. Chairs and cloth can be used to create a bus.

- You may wish to make an obstacle course. Example: Using cloth, hoops, furniture, equipment - a landscape can be created. Tunnels to crawl through, beams to balance upon, obstacles to be leapt over.

Often the challenge for the TAF is to slow the action (delay gratification) and maintain the dramatic tension, thus truly enabling children to experience the effects of their choices.

Work to resolve the drama, bringing it to a satisfactory conclusion

A drama does not necessarily have to have one ending, but it is important for all involved to feel a sense of closure. Multiple endings can be tried. Reflection and evaluation play an important role in drama. The children should be encouraged to consider the consequences of the choices they make. Visual art activities and rituals can be effective ways of children sharing their understandings. Simple songs and chants can also be effective ways to bookend a drama and the removal of imaginary garments can help children make the transition from the imaginary to reality.

Foot stories

These stories owe their origin to Anne Green Gilbert's foot stories and the work of Helen Landalf and Pamela Gerke. These 'full bodied' movement stories are all designed to take place in self-space. That is, they are non-locomotive. They are a great way to:

- Actively engage children in storytelling

- Burn off energy in restricted spaces

- Extend and develop children's flexibility, strength, balance, postural alignment and coordination

They involve a narrative, which is 'illustrated' by a series of floor and/or standing stretches. The characters, represented by the feet, are usually two animals. I have chosen geckos because they are native animals to both New Zealand and Australia, but you may choose different animals. These stretches are a mixture of yoga postures and sports/dance exercises.

Although these stories can be shared with a child on a one-on-one basis, they are best shared when the group forms a circle. Children should remove their shoes and socks. All feet should be pointing towards the centre of the circle. Children should be sitting in an upright position with their legs stretched straight in front of them. Each child will need space behind, in front and to either side of them. The adult narrating the story should sit with the children in the circle and demonstrate the stretches as she narrates the story.

Once children become familiar with the frame of the stories, they will start making their own contributions and suggestions, which can be included. You may choose to go on and create various foot stories of your own, choosing your own animals as main characters.

Resources, references and recommendations

Braiding Sweetgrass: Indigenous Wisdom, Scientific Knowledge and the Teachings of Plants by Robin Wall Kimmerer, Penguin, 2020

A Tohunga's Natural World: Plants, Gardening and Food by Paul Moon, David Ling Publishing Limited, 2005

The Spell of the Sensuous: Perception and Language in a More-Than-Human World by David Abram, Vintage, 1996

Scatterlings: Getting Claimed in the Age of Amnesia by Martin Shaw, White Cloud Press, 2016

Matariki: The Star of the Year by Dr Rangi Matamua, Huia Publishers, 2017

Celebrating the Southern Seasons: Rituals for Aotearoa by Juliet Batten (revised edition), Random House NZ, 2005

Sun, Moon, and Stars: Seasonal celebrations for children and families by Juliet Batten, Ishtar Books, 2020

Dancing with the Seasons By Juliet Batten, Ishtar Books, 2010

Active Hope: How to Face the Mess We're in without Going Crazy by Joanna Macy, (revised edition) New World Library, 2022

Additional Resources & activities for te tau hou Māori (new year) and stars

For a general overview of Matariki watch the videos on Dr Rangi Matamua's Youtube channel

A downloadable Matariki activity book is available from the Te Papa website at tepapa.govt.nz

The story of Matariki and Six Sisters, by Ngāti Toa Rangatira is available as fantastic video on Youtube, posted by Te Papa

A video tutorial on making whetū (stars) from harakeke (flax) is available from the Manaaki Whenua land care website: landcareresearch. co.nz

A kite making resource with additional links is available from the Christchurch City library website: my.christchurchcitylibraries.com

Additional links to fire stories

Aotearoa/New Zealand
The story of how Maui brought fire to the world is available from the Ministry of Education website at tiki.org.nz

Australia
A downloadable PDF of traditional Aboriginal fire stories, produced by Fire and Rescue New South Wales is available online.

General
A good overview of fire and folklore can be found on the Learn Religions website: at learnreligions.com

Additional links to bat resources

Aotearoa/New Zealand

Pekapeka action song by Tanya Batt and Peter Forster is available, among other videos, from Tanya's Vimeo channel at vimeo.com/tanyabatt

BushTellyTV Youtube channel has a great clip about pekapeka.

Fleabite Youtube channel has a great clip by Robin Nathan on 'Bat Fly'.

Department of Conservation youtube channel also has some great bat resources.

The Extinction Channel has fantatstic clip on youtube about the Giant Burrowing Bat.

Australian Bats

ausbats.org.au and allaboutbats.org.au have some great bat related info.

Author Bio

Tanya Batt is a seed sower, a word warbler and story stitcher who channelled her childhood propensity for talking and her love of growing things into a real 'imaginary job'. Her home is on the Awaawaroa Bay Eco Village on Waiheke Island, Aotearoa, New Zealand. Stories have kept her curious, putting food on her table, a roof over her head and enabled her to travel the world and share her mahi for more than thirty years. She is the creative director of the 'Once Upon An Island Charitable Trust' that uses storytelling for community building, environmental and cultural education. You can find out more about Tanya and browse resources at imagined-worlds.net

Artist Bio

Kristy Barlow is a New Zealand illustrator based in Canada who specializes in children's illustration. She has always been drawn to creative expression as both a form of communication and as an indulgence of the imagination - whether it be through drawing, painting, writing, music, fashion, or dance. Her artwork is a representation of how she experiences the world; with a finely tuned sensitivity to the details that make up our beautifully diverse world. She believes our differences should be celebrated and nurtured, which is habitually reflected throughout her illustrations. www.kristybarlow.com